FAITH AND FIRE

Elijah

PRISCILLA SHIRER

LifeWay Press®
Nashville, Tennessee

Published by LifeWay Press® • ©2020 Priscilla Shirer

ISBN 978-1-0877-1542-1
Item 005826639
Dewey decimal classification: 221.92
Subject heading: FAITH / ELIJAH, PROPHET / BIBLE. O.T. 1 KINGS—STUDY AND TEACHING

To order additional copies of this resource, write LifeWay Church Resources Customer Service; One LifeWay Plaza; Nashville, TN 37234-0113; Fax orders to 615.251.5933; call toll-free 800.458.2772; email orderentry@lifeway.com; order online at LifeWay.com; or visit the LifeWay Christian Store serving you.

Printed in the United States of America.

Adult Ministry Publishing, LifeWay Church Resources, One LifeWay Plaza, Nashville, TN 37234-0152

EDITORIAL TEAM, LIFEWAY WOMEN PUBLISHING

Becky Loyd
Director, LifeWay Women

Tina Boesch
Manager, LifeWay Women Bible Studies

Sarah Doss
Editorial Project Leader, LifeWay Women Bible Studies

Lawrence Kimbrough
Content Editor

Lindsey Bush
Production Editor

Lauren Ervin
Graphic Designer

Contents

ABOUT THE AUTHOR

Whether in packed-out arenas or intimate Bible study group settings, Priscilla Shirer's influence has been steady and trusted. For more than twenty years her voice has resonated with raw power and unapologetic clarity to teach God's Word. Through her speaking ministry, best-selling books, and Bible studies, or even on a movie screen, Priscilla's primary ambition is clear—to lift up Jesus and equip His children to live victoriously.

Priscilla has been married to Jerry Shirer for twenty-one years. Together they lead Going Beyond Ministries, which exists to serve believers across the spectrum of the church. To date, the ministry has released more than a dozen video-driven studies for women and teens on a myriad of biblical characters (like Jonah and Gideon), as well as topical studies on *Discerning the Voice of God,* *The Armor of God,* and others. Priscilla has also written a fiction series called *The Prince Warriors,* in addition to award-winning books like *Fervent* and *The Resolution for Women.*

She and her family make their home near Dallas, Texas, where between her writing and studying, Priscilla spends her days trying to clean up after (and satisfy the appetites of) her three rapidly growing teenage sons.

INTRODUCTION

It was 2014 when I first started studying and teaching on the life and ministry of Elijah. After sharing parts of his narrative in bits and pieces, I knew I had to write about him one day. Little did I know the resource you're holding in your hands would take another seven years to materialize.

The reasons are many. Several other projects elbowed their way in, taking priority and pushing this one to the background. The busyness of my sons' lives and my involvement with them accelerated exponentially as they blossomed into young manhood. But most of the delay came from a number of unexpected, back-to-back tragedies (I'll tell you about them soon), each of which pushed the pause button on my life, forcing me to sit still for long stretches of emotional and physical recovery.

Before any of this happened, I'd felt compelled to start keeping a journal specifically for the purpose of chronicling my own spiritual journey—keeping track of God's faithfulness, recording my raw conversations with Him, tracing the often imperceptible shifts that His Spirit was working in me at the time. I'm so glad I did. Because while I'll never know my Father's reasons for all these delays—or for the losses, hurts, and challenges that precipitated them—I do know they were, at least in part, for you.

In flipping back through those handwritten entries, reliving the many things that God reframed and refreshed in my heart, I couldn't help noticing how His work in me had added layers of heartfelt depth that would've been missing from these lessons if I'd stayed on my earlier timetable. In His providence all these delays have become detours, aligning you and me in this current season of our lives. I'm convinced God has infused this work with a power that only comes through brokenness, weakness, and struggle. And I'm praying the proof of this holy impact is somehow reflected on each page—that you don't only learn something but experience something.

A renewed faith. A fresh fire.

Our world, more than ever, is longing for the sons and daughters of God to arise in the spirit of Elijah. That's why I think this might just be the perfect time for our paths to cross here, so that God can comfort you, strengthen you, encourage you, and prepare you for the Mount Carmels that lie ahead.

Welcome, my friend—I've been waiting for you. And it's been a long time coming.

Gilead

THE STARTING POINT

FAITH: COMMITTING TO GOD'S PROCESS

WEEK ONE

THE START OF A PROCESS

Everybody wants the Mount _____. We want the flashy display of God's _____ in our lives.

And yet in the shadow of these magnificent events is a _____. There's always a _____.

We've got to _____ _____ to go through the process.

Are you willing to do _____ _____ _____ to get _____ _____ _____?

First and Second Kings shows a time when idolatry was not just _____, and not just _____, but was actually legislated.

Elijah means: _____ is _____.

He didn't just say Yahweh is God; he said _____ is _____ _____.

Then he said to King Ahab, Yahweh _____.

Here's how God was going to remind Ahab that He alone is alive: "There shall be neither _____ nor rain these years, except by my _____."

Not only was the drought a judgment against the people's _____, but it was also a specific indictment against the _____ of Baal.

We can have the courage to rise up in the _____ of Elijah, and to make sure we are God's mouthpiece in this _____.

Video and audio sessions available for purchase and rent at LifeWay.com/Elijah.

7

THE REAL DEAL

"After you have suffered for a little while, the God of all grace, who called you to His eternal glory in Christ, will Himself perfect, confirm, strengthen and establish you."

1 PETER 5:10

I was scrolling mindlessly through my Instagram® feed one day when a particular image snagged my attention. Startled me. Sort of grossed me out, to tell you the truth, peeking out from underneath my paused thumb. You know how you can see something that's a little disturbing to you, a little provocative, and even though you really want to turn away, you somehow can't seem to stop looking? It was kind of like that.

Half of the image showed a beautifully poised, perfectly arched ballerina's foot. Smooth, elegant, and dainty. Her cream-colored slipper fit like a satin glove, along with a silk ribbon woven meticulously up her ankle, completing the classic look. It was everything you'd expect. Like a piece of fine art. So pretty. So precise.

But then—the *other* side.

And this other side told a much different story. The real story.

Directly next to the dancer's lovely, shapely right foot was her *other* foot. Her *bare* foot. Without its slipper. And the contrast was visibly striking. Whole nails were missing. Several of the knuckles, swollen red, were bandaged, blistered, or bleeding. Fragments of old, stained gauze remained stuck to oozing sores. Knobs of contorted, misshapen bones bulged grotesquely beneath the skin.

And along with the picture ran the following caption, or words similar to this effect:

EVERYONE WANTS THE GLORY, BUT FEW ARE WILLING TO PAY THE PRICE REQUIRED TO GET IT.

Well, ain't that the truth.

We want the highlight reel, not the practice session. Not the years of hard work. Not the consistent pattern of sacrifice. Not the going over and over again of the same, repeated steps and movements. The stretching. The soreness. The getting out of bed on cold, sleepy mornings. The slow, slow walk of patience, whatever it takes to get it right.

Truth be told, when we scroll through our social media feeds, we only want to see the ballerina slipper. It's prettier and more palatable. The worn parts, the beat-up parts, douse the wildfire of our romantic imagination. Reality is too much for us to deal with. A close look at the hours of preparation, the years of hard work, and the grueling cost required to get there are not what we came to see. So we conveniently ignore that part.

If we're honest with ourselves and each other, that's how we tend to read the Bible too.

When you think of these Old Testament personalities, what highlights immediately come to mind? Write your thoughts below.

NOAH	
ABRAHAM	
MOSES	
SAMUEL	
ESTHER	

"No discipline seems enjoyable at the time, but painful. Later on, however, it yields the peaceful fruit of righteousness to those who have been trained by it."

HEBREWS 12:11, CSB

Now think of someone who's living today, even if it's someone you may not know personally, whose life you admire from afar. What are some of the character highlights you've seen in him or her that impress you the most?

Several years ago I took on the task of reading the Bible through in a year. Frankly, I found it a bit overwhelming. (Wrangling three small children at the time probably had a little something to do with it.) Maybe I needed the two-year plan, where I could take it more slowly and digest things a little more fully that way. Yet I distinctly remember, when I came to Elijah's narrative in 1 Kings that year, how I felt completely consumed by the startling boldness of his faith, especially the one big highlight that stands out from his story: *Mount Carmel.*

Go ahead and turn to 1 Kings 18:19-39. (It's a pretty sizable portion of Scripture. But exciting. Lots of action. You'll love it.) As you're reading, list here all the elements from this holy encounter that demonstrate the prophet's faith, courage, commitment, and prayer.

- Now look back through the things you wrote down. Which of them clearly demonstrate his *faith* at work? (Put an "F" beside those.)
- His *courage* against opposition? (Mark those with a "C.")
- The *boldness* of his witness? ("B" of course)
- His keen ability to *pray*? ("P")

With all this in mind, imagine if Elijah were sitting beside you right now. What are the top three questions you'd like to ask him about his memories from that day?

1.

2.

3.

As I think through the conversation I'd like to have with Elijah, I try to picture how he might interact with me. While I'd be all zeroed in on the spectacular moments of the story, I wonder if he'd intentionally point to other things—simpler, more foundational things, even difficult things that made up the underbelly of his journey with God. I wonder if he'd accentuate those quieter happenings from earlier in his life, in passages preceding 1 Kings 18, verses that are filled with refining and pruning.

These encounters leading up to Mount Carmel were precisely where the Holy Spirit seemed to shine a spotlight for me as I was reading. They captured me. They tell us Elijah didn't just show up out of thin air knowing exactly what to do and exactly how to do it. All that faith, all that courage, all that boldness and confidence in prayer—all that *fire!*—didn't just happen. Each of these impressive strengths we see in him had been fortified by earlier struggles, during earlier challenges, through earlier forays into trust and obedience.

This moment of biblical proportions, high atop Mount Carmel, followed a much less public process that God had begun in him years before—a process that is already happening in you as well, which your loving Father will continue to develop throughout this study—a progression of development that I hope you'll begin to recognize and value more than ever before.

I'm assuming you're here with me in these pages because we both want what Elijah had.

We want:

- faith, courage, and boldness,
- a prayer life that pushes back the darkness,
- character that possesses an unflinching backbone,
- a holy conviction that doesn't bow to popular opinion.

We want to be:

- brimming over with the fullness of God's Spirit and power,
- brave enough to speak truth to authority with love and grace,
- singularly focused, inspiring others' allegiance to the one true God,
- people who leave behind a lasting impact on future generations.

These are incredibly noble aspirations. But the question for us remains:

ARE WE WILLING TO DO WHAT ELIJAH DID TO GET WHAT ELIJAH GOT?

What excites you the most as you contemplate that question?

What scares you the most about it? What do you find the most challenging about it?

You have no idea how I wish I could lean into your Bible study book right now and see how you've prayerfully responded. Then I'd move out of the way and let you peer into mine. Because right here is where the battle is about to be waged—on the thin edge that exists between our eager anticipation about the next level where God is calling us and the prickling fear we sometimes feel about what it will cost us to get there.

In a sentence or two, summarize what each of the following passages declares as being the potential cost of building your . . .

FAITH (Heb. 11:13-16)	
COURAGE (1 Cor. 2:1-5)	
BOLD WITNESS (Luke 21:12-19)	
PRAYER POWER (Matt. 6:5-6)	

"Blessed is a man who perseveres under trial; for once he has been approved, he will receive the crown of life which the Lord has promised to those who love Him."

JAMES 1:12

In Hebrews 11, I see faith heroes who didn't make comfort their primary life ambition.

How might this refocusing away from comfort and toward calling be part of your process?

In 1 Corinthians 2, I see a man who was unmotivated by cultural acceptance, indifferent to the approval of his peers, uninterested in impressing others with his own ability.

How might being less concerned with public perception be part of your process?

In Luke 21, I see Jesus' disciples being challenged not to avoid persecution but be prepared to face it—and be testimonies of God's glory in the middle of it.

How might learning to endure opposition be part of your process?

In Matthew 6, I see crowds of religious people being instructed by Jesus to dismantle the veneer of pious tradition, exchanging it for real, authentic, fervent relationship with Him.

How might developing a deeper purity and fervency in prayer be part of your process?

Hear me, sister, and hear me good. The process of working toward these goals will not be easy. In fact, I can assure you, it will step on your toes now and again. But still, it will all be worth it. It's the pattern I've detected in the men and women of God whom I most admire. People who live in passionate relationship with Him. People who stand strong in the midst of adversity. People who experience Him in a real and living way. People whose prayers pulsate with power. People who hear God's voice and see His activity. People who are unapologetic about their faith.

Let me tell you what they've been doing all these years while everybody else was lacing up their ballerina slippers and adjusting the lighting for their staged social images. They've been in the darkroom of development:

- *dedicating* time in the presence of God;

- *devoting* their talents and treasures for His use and purposes;

- *prioritizing* what the world mocks and minimizes;

- *sacrificing* their own selfish desires and ambitions;

- *feeling* frequently marginalized and excluded;

- *breaking* off any unhealthy relationships;

- *upholding* their daily spiritual disciplines;

- *daring* to risk bold allegiance to His Word;

- *resisting* a lifestyle of legalistic, condemning perfectionism;

- *receiving* each day a continuous stream of God's grace;

- *refusing* political correctness over righteousness;

- *reaching* out to the weak and disenfranchised;

- *believing* God for more and more; and

- *praying* the bold prayers to prove it.

They've committed themselves to the things God's people do in order to receive what only God can give. It's taken patience and practice, waiting and endurance. It's taken time. They've got the bumps, bruises, scars, and injuries to show for it. But only those willing to investigate more deeply—like you? like me?—will get a chance to see and learn from the processes they've endured.

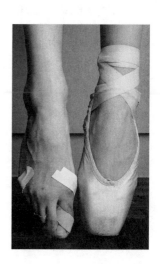

That's what we're going to do with Elijah over the next few weeks.

JUST LIKE ME

"Friends, why are you doing this?
We too are only human, like you."

ACTS 14:15a, NIV

Legendary. Larger than life. A "colossus amongst ordinary men"[1] is how Elijah is described by many scholars who have written about his place in biblical history.

The Bible sets him beside Moses as the primary prophetic figure of the Old Testament and uses him as a point of spiritual reference throughout the New Testament, centuries after he lived. He seems almost super-human, right? An exception to the rule instead of an example to which we can aspire.

> James wrote to a community of Jewish Christians who were being persecuted for their faith and as a result had been "scattered abroad" (1:1, NKJV) out of Jerusalem. They were enduring intense external persecution along with internal battles of the flesh—anger, vengeance, and the temptation to sin.

Yet before we even let that doubt begin to blossom in our minds, the writer of the Book of James tells us something we all need to remember.

Turn to James 5:17 in your own Bible. In the space below, write just the opening phrase of it—the part up through the first comma or so.

Consider the context of James's writing. Why do you think, when writing about the power of prayer, he was inspired by the Holy Spirit to include this comment to his original audience, people who held Elijah in such high esteem?

Why is this point important to readers like us today?

As I mentioned, I tend to put other people on a pedestal—people who appear to experience God and exercise their faith at a level that seems beyond my reach, people for whom He appears to be present, active, and available in ways that apparently don't apply to the rest of us.

I've noticed many reasons why we all tend toward this. I'll mention two of them, then I'll let you personally and prayerfully consider them: (1) *the pedestal creates a safe distance between us.* It makes me think the reason there's such a difference in how they live, versus how I live, is because they're just so different from me to begin with. And so (2) *the pedestal allows me to set a lower bar for myself.* Since living like them is so far above me, I feel like I can afford to placate my own laziness, my complacency, my lack of spiritual sacrifice and diligence. After all, who am I? I'm not even in their league. They're in a whole other category.

I'm just an ordinary person.

But the results of the pedestal can be devastating, both for them and for me.

For them, because the pedestal ascribes unrealistic standards to them. By idolizing someone, I run the risk of crippling them. I contribute to the pressure they feel for maintaining perfect performance. I make it harder for them to freely explore the far reaches of their faith, out where they risk exposing their frailty by leaning on the grace and goodness of God rather than their own awesomeness.

For me, because the pedestal leaves me open to being hurt and disillusioned. People are going to make mistakes, I don't care who they are or how admirable their relationship with the Lord. Even heroes will falter and stumble along the way, which we'll see in Elijah toward the end of our study. I do a disservice to them, as well as to myself, when I hold them to a level of perfection that belongs only to Christ, who alone is the Perfect One. I need to let everyone else off the hook for not being Him, because there's a good reason why they're not. They're just ordinary people.

I asked you yesterday to think about the character highlights you admire in others. Consider whether you've inadvertently put any of those people on a pedestal. Today I want you to list just their names. Do any other people come to mind as well? List their names here too.

How would you describe the self-perceived *distance* between you and them?

How does the high standard you've imposed on them translate to a *lower standard* for yourself?

How are you being *unrealistic* in the performance you expect of them?

How have you been *hurt* or *disappointed* by them because of your own unrealistic expectations for how they should live?

We get ourselves (and others) into so much needless trouble when we insist on building these pedestals for people who, underneath it all, are *Just. Like. Us.*

Just like Elijah.

I don't know if what I'm about to say will come as a surprise, and I don't want to spoil some of the lessons we'll study down the line. But as a bit of a preview for what the Bible is going to show us about the things Elijah faced in life and how he dealt with them, prepare for these realities:

- We're going to see Elijah hungry, tired, and irritable.

- We're going to see Elijah discouraged and despondent.

- We're going to see Elijah doubtful and insecure.

In other words, we are going to see Elijah as human.

The original Greek word used in James 5:17 to describe Elijah is ***anthropos*** [AHN-thro-pahs], which refers to all beings participating within the human race.

Yes, the great prophet Elijah had his emotional tailspins. *We'll see them.* The great prophet Elijah was an expert at wallowing in self-pity. *We'll see it.* The great prophet Elijah failed and flailed and needed God the same way we fail and flail and need God ourselves. *Get ready to see that too.* Even after the adrenaline rush of watching God's fire fall from heaven at Mount Carmel, and then actively participating in bringing his enemies to a fitting end, Elijah crashed into an abyss of exhaustion and fatigue. And fear. And paranoia. He ran. He was done.

So while Elijah is an example for us, he is not an exception to us. We must resist our tendency to venerate him and other biblical heroes like him. None of the biblical heroes were intended to be an exception; they are all meant to be examples to us of what happens when an ordinary life intersects with an extraordinary God.

Prepare yourself to look at Elijah this way, and then see what the Holy Spirit reveals to you in the process.

Based on some of the "coming attractions" that I told you we can expect to see in Elijah's life, let me ask you to be introspective for a moment. In what specific ways do you deal with:

- **Insecurity?**

- **Irritability?**

- **Discouragement?**

- **Loss of perspective?**

How does it encourage you to realize someone as epic as Elijah could feel and exhibit and battle with some of these same things?

Here's how it helps me. It tells me Elijah's limitations, weaknesses, and emotional quirks didn't scare God off or disqualify him from serving God in a mighty way. God *knew* all these tendencies in Elijah. He factored all of them into the unique plan He'd designed for Elijah's life. He didn't ignore His prophet's needs and neuroses. He worked with them; He made use of them in showing His care for Elijah, as well as showing what He can accomplish in each of us despite our human imperfections.

Looking at the previous paragraph, underline the portions that encourage you to free yourself from feelings of self-condemnation or uselessness.

Let's make a couple of commitments right here, based on the premise of James 5:17.

First, let's quit trying to hide our humanity—from God, from others, even from ourselves. Elijah's humanity—his *anthropos*—was not a liability to God's purposes. Neither is yours. Being human never prevented God from using yielded servants, like you and I can be, to do what He's called us to accomplish.

In what clever ways do you attempt to paint a veneer that masks your human limitations, your private outbursts, the realness of your own struggles with living by faith?

Why do you think you place such importance, if you do, on keeping up a façade that impresses others or somehow garners God's approval?

Second, let's quit treating other people as superhuman. And if learning it from an Old Testament prophet is not enough, let's seal today's lesson in our hearts with a quick look at a New Testament apostle.

Paul and Barnabas were preaching in a certain city one day where a crippled man was in the audience, someone who'd been "lame from his mother's womb, who had never walked" (Acts 14:8). Paul recognized the man's plight and perceived he had faith that God could make him well. "Stand upright on your feet," Paul shouted to him across the way in a loud, commanding voice. The Bible says the man "leaped up and began to walk" (v. 10).

"Elijah was a man with a nature like ours, and he prayed earnestly that it would not rain, and it did not rain on the earth for three years and six months."

JAMES 5:17

Turn to Acts 14:11. What did the crowd start saying about Paul and Barnabas when they saw the evidence of this miracle?

Read verse 12. What two names did they ascribe to them?

Read verse 13. How did the priest of Zeus want to honor them?

Read verse 14. How did Paul and Barnabas rightly react to all this?

Read verse 15. What phrase in here sounds a whole lot like James 5:17?

There it is again—*anthropos*. Like Paul. Like Elijah.

Like us.

Flip back a few pages to that list of names you wrote down earlier. As you reflect on these individuals and how they've influenced your life, do something for me. Thank the Lord for them. Thank Him for working through each of these people, through their humanness (which you know is underneath all that impressiveness), and for using their lives as such moving examples of His grace and power. Ask the Lord to sustain them as they seek to honor Him.

And then thank the Lord for something else. Say it something like this:

Thank You, Lord, that because they are human beings, just as I am:

- *I, too, can experience that kind of intimacy with You;*

- *I, too, can hear Your voice clearly and obey courageously;*

- *I, too, can share my faith without sugarcoating it or being ashamed;*

- *I, too, can stand alone, knowing You're with me when my trust is in You;*

- *I, too, can serve the needs of others, even when my own needs are unmet;*

- *I, too, can pray with forgiven confidence in You and Your promises;*

- *I, too, can be used by You to turn people's hearts back to faith;*

- *I, too, can stare into uncertainty and know You'll never fail.*

Amen.

And do you know what I see, as you sit there, or kneel there, praying like that?

I see a lot of Elijah in you.

THESE ARE THE DAYS OF ELIJAH

"You have observed the statutes of Omri and all the practices of Ahab's house; you have followed their traditions. Therefore I will give you over to ruin and your people to derision; you will bear the scorn of nations."

MICAH 6:16, NIV

My nephew Kamden is a five-year-old ball of human fire, filled with more energy and precocious mischievousness than maybe any kid I've ever met. The fourth of five children, he is constantly trying to press the limits, to push past the boundaries. If not for the watchful oversight of his parents—my brother Jonathan and his wife, Kanika—there'd be no barrier between himself and the dangers of, say, a swimming pool, a crowded intersection, a threatening animal. You get the picture? This is the reason why one of Kamden's frequent locations is right smack-dab in the middle of his father's lap, being lovingly and securely held down for his own protection.

Sometimes, though, I've watched Jonathan let him go—not because he didn't want to protect his son, but because he decided in the moment that Kamden would learn better through painful experience.

On one occasion when Kamden was about two, Jonathan was helping him down a flight of stairs, holding tightly to his hand. But Kamden was squirming, fighting to free himself, insisting on making it to the bottom without help. When they finally got to the last step, Jonathan gave Kamden what he wanted. He let go of his hand, despite what everyone else besides Kamden knew for sure would happen next. His little two-year-old legs weren't long enough to steady his weight from one riser to the next, so he took a little spill. Not enough to injure him, but enough to teach him this valuable lesson: *My father knows best.*

Our relationship with our heavenly Father is much the same. Many times, in order to keep us protected, He holds us close. He hems us in.

But at other times, still motivated by that same great love, He releases us to our own demands. He lets go. And we learn the harder way.

Read the two passages below. One speaks of God holding us close, and the other speaks of God letting us go. Beside each, write the key phrases that point to these realities and minister to you personally.

• Isaiah 41:8-13

• Psalm 81:8-14

Recall a time when you experienced God's care in either form:

• By how He did *not* release you to go your own way.

• By how He *did* release you to go your own way.

Looking back, how did you see God's love reflected in each case?

How have you found each dynamic necessary (or at least effective) in reminding you to remain surrendered and submitted to your Father's leadership?

Now let's connect all of this to our study. In 1 Kings 17, as Elijah first comes into view, the sense we get from Scripture is that God had released the nation to the consequences of their duplicitous choices. Sort of like my nephew Kamden, the Israelites had stiffened their necks against God's protective authority. Progressively over a number of decades, they'd refused a posture of surrender toward His divine care and guidance. Even worse, they'd turned their backs on Him, had refused His loving advances, and had chased the wicked lifestyles and allegiances encouraged by their rebellious, godless leaders.

It was now somewhere around 870 BC—significant because it had been no more than a hundred years since King Solomon had led the people in a national dedication of their newly completed temple. The contrast between the two time periods—which was a conceivable human lifetime—could not be more striking. A quick glimpse can give us an eye-opening view of how severely the moral compass had shifted.

> "All the sons of Israel, seeing the fire come down and the glory of the LORD upon the house, bowed down on the pavement with their faces to the ground, and they worshiped and gave praise to the LORD, saying, 'Truly He is good, truly His lovingkindness is everlasting.'"
>
> 2 CHRONICLES 7:3

Open your Bible to 2 Chronicles 7:1-3, where King Solomon had just completed his powerful prayer at the dedication ceremony. What does this moment tell you about:

• The spiritual leadership of Israel during this time?

• The blessing and favor of their God upon them?

• The spiritual posture of the people in relationship to God?

Think about the decline of cultural norms during your own lifetime. Or talk with someone you know whose lifetime already spans eighty years or more. Between the two of you, what are some of the distinctive moral and spiritual differences you've seen in the cultural climate between then and now?

There were likely people still alive in Elijah's day who'd been present at Solomon's grand dedication of the temple, even if just as little kids. Many could remember going up to Jerusalem to worship during Israel's annual feasts. They knew what it meant to be led well, to live in a culture where honoring God was the norm, where they were surrounded by others who agreed with them that marginalizing Yahweh was not in their best interest. They knew how it looked when God dispensed His blessing, grace, and glory to them in unmistakable ways. They knew what being held closely by Him felt like.

But over the course of eight decades in Israel, spanning the reigns of six different kings, the God-honoring families who once esteemed Him had incrementally relaxed their commitments. They'd departed from the singular worship of Yahweh. They'd welcomed idolatrous activity into their lives as an accepted practice.

Look up the following passages from 1 Kings, summarizing the reigns of the six kings of Israel—the Northern Kingdom—following Solomon's reign. Fill in the blanks with either the king's name or a brief description of his leadership.

Remember, the nation split in two after Solomon's death. The two tribes of the Southern Kingdom were known as Judah; the ten tribes of the Northern Kingdom were known as Israel.

VERSE	KING	DESCRIPTION
12:28-32	Jeroboam	
15:25-26		"did evil . . . walked in the way of his father"
15:33-34		"walked in the way of Jeroboam . . . made Israel sin"
16:8-10	Elah	
16:15-19		"reigned seven days . . . evil in the sight of the LORD"
16:23-25	Omri	

Now we come to Ahab, who was the king of Israel when Elijah emerged onto the scene. Ahab, the Bible says, "walked in all the way of Jeroboam" (1 Kings 16:26). This comment compels us to discover what former King Jeroboam did.

After the nation split, the people of Israel continued making the long trek to the temple in Jerusalem for worship. But since the temple was now technically located in another kingdom, Jeroboam decided to compromise on God's laws, presumably to make worship more convenient for his subjects, to save them that lengthy trip. He hoped by this policy of practicality to keep his people close to home, cementing their loyalty to him instead of to their brothers in Judah.

> Jeroboam's actions were a flagrant example of *syncretism* (SINK-re-tism), the practice of absorbing conflicting religious views into one cosmopolitan belief system, until all roads lead to God, and nothing really means anything.

After discussions with his advisors, what did Jeroboam set up in the northern cities (1 Kings 12:28-29)?

Whom did he install as religious leaders there (1 Kings 12:31)?

Jeroboam combined the worship of Yahweh with idolatry. He didn't yet make Israel's allegiance to God *defunct*, but he made it *divided*. And whenever loyalties are divided, that's where *decline* always begins.

Ruling in this way—in "the way of Jeroboam"—was a common descriptor for *all* the kings of Israel. But for Ahab, it was just the beginning. He considered what the previous kings had done in dishonoring God "a trivial thing" (1 Kings 16:31). Ahab "did evil in the sight of the LORD more than all who were before him" (v. 30).

For instance, he erected an altar to Baal for the Israelites to worship—not in *addition* to God, but in *place* of God (v. 32). He added to this blasphemy by making an image of Asherah, the goddess mother of Baal (v. 33). Then in complete disregard for the law of God, he married a pagan wife, Jezebel, daughter of a pagan king. She insisted the worship of Baal become the sum total of Israel's religious life, effectively criminalizing the worship of Yahweh. Israelite culture was no longer *divided* but now *demonic* and *degenerate*.

In another snapshot of Ahab's disregard for God's Word, compare the activity described in 1 Kings 16:34 with the prohibition laid out in Joshua 6:26. In your study, consider these questions:

• What tragedies befell Jericho's new developer?

• What should this have brought to Ahab's mind?

> "You shall not intermarry with them; you shall not give your daughters to their sons, nor shall you take their daughters for your sons. For they will turn your sons away from following Me to serve other gods; then the anger of the LORD will be kindled against you and He will quickly destroy you."
>
> **DEUTERONOMY 7:3-4**

• What should he have done about it?

The spiritual indifference and negligence of all the kings of Israel since Solomon had been offensive to God. Year after year. Decade after decade. But the sharpness of Ahab's departure from worship of the one true God grieved the Lord even more. And at this low ebb of the declining arc, God did what fathers sometimes have to do.

He let go.

And like it or not, God does so even now. The sad reality is that our current culture is experiencing some of the same effects of this divine relinquishing.

Read Romans 1:18-32. I know it's a tough passage, and a lengthy one. But the gravity of it is too critical to shortcut. As you read, underline in your Bible anything that stands out as being particularly convicting to you.

How is it hauntingly descriptive of the culture in Elijah's day? In our day?

"Therefore God gave them over in the lusts of their hearts to impurity, so that their bodies would be dishonored among them" (v. 24).

Even in this hard reading, don't overlook God's desire to comfort, to *hold us close*. In verse 20, we see a loving God taking the initiative to make known His invisible presence, to establish relationship with people. He doesn't want to be hidden and unknown. He has revealed Himself in creation so clearly that even those who aren't seeking Him or wanting Him can be captivated by His majesty and power, His beauty and tenderness, as seen in the world around them. In fact, the evidence is so conspicuous that those who don't believe are held responsible for ignoring it because in self-deceit they have willingly suppressed the mountain of evidence.

"For this reason God gave them over to degrading passions" (v. 26a).

But we are simultaneously confronted. We see Him *let us go*. When people foolishly declare there is no God, or when they dishonor Him by refusing to acknowledge Him or give Him due reverence, He eventually lets go. When people hate the things God has called good, or love the things He's called evil, He finally just lets them have what they want, as well as the consequences that come with it.

"And just as they did not see fit to acknowledge God any longer, God ← gave them over to a depraved mind" (v. 28a).

Zero in on the verses from Romans 1 reprinted in the margin. Underline each place where it says "God gave them over."

What do these verses specify as the results of God's divine relinquishing? What did they experience after He gave them over?

- Dishonored _____

- Degrading _____

- Depraved _____

As children of God—saved, redeemed, and forgiven—the status of our relationship with Him never changes, just as Kamden's relationship to his daddy never changes. But it doesn't mean our *experience* with Him won't change if we persist in refusing to honor Him. He will sometimes choose tough, letting-go love as the best option for reminding us that the ingredients we're mixing into our lives are a recipe for disaster.

These were the days of Elijah. Days of experiencing God's letting go. But just when Israel was spiraling downward, God was stirring up a representative in the rugged mountains of Gilead who would call His people back.

Elijah was coming.

THE PROCESS OF PREPARATION

"Elijah the Tishbite, who was of the settlers of Gilead . . ."

1 KINGS 17:1a

Shawna is one of my dearest friends, a beautiful ray of sunlight in my life. She's honest; she's cheerful; she's generous. She's real. Whenever I see her, I can't help smiling from ear to ear. As a licensed counselor, she's the kind of person who can minster to people from all walks of life about a myriad of issues and concerns.

We've known each other a long time and have basically raised our children together, offering advice back and forth to one another through their toddler and teenage years. Her oldest, Joshua, is now a cadet at West Point. Her middle child, daughter Elyana, graduated as valedictorian of her high school class. And her youngest, Noah, is a bright, handsome, soft-spoken middle schooler whose smile, I promise, would light up your whole life.

But before these three came along, Shawna and her husband endured the tormenting grief of having to bury their first two children. With each pregnancy, the doctor prescribed long stints of bed rest in order to keep the baby protected in her womb. Yet each time she delivered them both early. They were too small, too weak, to survive on their own. So she held them and wept over them, watching them take their first (and last) staccato breaths. First it was Grace, and then it was Caleb. It was never anything but heartbreaking.

Why would the Lord allow this? *I don't know.*

But I can tell you this: whenever I see Shawna speaking to a young woman whose heart has been broken by the loss of a child—when I see her folding that woman's trembling hands inside her own—that's when I see her living in the sweet spot of her ministry and effectiveness. Does it negate the pain, grief, and hardship that she and her husband faced? Would they want to live through it again or wish it on anyone else? Absolutely not. But seeing God redeem it this way—funneling it into heartfelt, compassionate ministry to others—does reframe their losses and give their grief purpose.

My friend has been *prepared* for these kinds of ministry moments. Prepared by what she's been through. Prepared by where she's come from.

This same sense of purpose and process is one of the undercurrents of Elijah's example.

Let's dig into 1 Kings 17. This is the first mention of the prophet in Scripture. And while we don't learn a lot about his background from the opening verse, we at least learn this:

- Elijah was a _____.

- His hometown was in an area called _____.

- And his first allegiance was to _____.

The exact location of *Tishbe*, despite being home to one of the greatest figures in all the Bible, cannot really be identified. Geologists and archaeologists have never been able to pinpoint it with any degree of accuracy. But *Gilead* comes with a bit more documentation. For the first time in our study, I want you to turn to the map I've provided for you on the inside back cover. Take a moment to survey it, making mental note of the places you know about, as well as the ones you're completely unfamiliar with. Now, look specifically at the area known as Gilead, east of the Jordan River. It actually shows up in the Bible on quite a few occasions.

From each of the following references, what interesting fact or happening can you connect with Gilead?

- Genesis 31:17-21

- Genesis 37:23-25

- Deuteronomy 34:1-4

Gilead was hill country, covered with dense forests and wild undergrowth. It was remote and uncivilized. Even its name—*Gilead*—means "rocky" or "rugged."

That's where Elijah was from. And that's who Elijah was. A mountain man. A tough, adventurous, free-ranging spirit. Picture him with callused hands and chipped, grubby fingernails. Picture him in scratchy, burlap-quality clothes. Picture his skin tanned and leathery, a thick and gnarled beard around his chin, his head topped by a matted stack of tousled, unruly hair.

Elijah wasn't groomed in the sophisticated manners and etiquette of the city. Elijah lacked classical education and social polish. His verbs and nouns didn't always agree. He wasn't brought up in echelons of society where he could earn the kinds of credentials and connections that paved his way to success.

Scholars believe he likely tended sheep on the heights of those lonely, uneven hillsides in Gilead.[2] It's where he learned to value and endure endless stretches of solitude and silence. It's where he had time to grow into a muscular, sinewy man with the tenacity it took to stave off predators and provide for his flocks.

Elijah came from a hard place. A rough place. An obscure place. The right place to be prepared for what God had in store for him.

"God is faithful, through whom you were called into fellowship with His Son, Jesus Christ our Lord."

1 CORINTHIANS 1:9

Think back to an earlier season of your life that perhaps was marked by hardship, challenge, loneliness, or obscurity. Record a few key words below that best describe that season for you.

Have you ever questioned why God allowed you to go through that season or to experience that difficulty? How so?

Looking at those experiences now from your current vantage point, how have they helped shape the way you think and feel about Him today?

The various events and circumstances that have contributed to your life up until this point have not been accidental. They've not been wasted parts of your process, even if they were difficult, even if they excluded you from certain privileges that in your estimation could have propelled you forward faster. Even the evil that's been done against you by people who intended you harm has not been a total loss. This doesn't excuse their wrongdoing, of course. It doesn't minimize the real pain they've caused you. But it does add a layer of perspective and hope. As Joseph could say, after being wrongfully treated by his brothers, after being unjustly enslaved and imprisoned in Egypt, "God meant it for good in order to bring about this present result" (Gen. 50:20).

For Elijah, the fact that he was raised in an uncouth environment; the fact that he wasn't brought up around more urbane, cultured tastes and people; the fact that he grew up at a distance from mass civilization; the fact that he had no lineage or pedigree even worth mentioning in the Bible. There was a reason for it.

All of it set the stage for the life God had planned for him.

God used it to give Elijah a clear, objective view of the duplicity that existed in the seat of Israel's power. By virtue of his outback upbringing, Elijah had not been tainted by living up close to the idolatrous influences of the city, nor dulled into spiritual apathy by its pious religious activity. Instead he was able to nurse a growing indignation about the declined moral state because he hadn't been absorbed into its fabric. Being from lowly regarded Gilead, Elijah was naturally unencumbered by the need to impress and please others, which made him an ideal mouthpiece for delivering the righteous message God wanted him to convey.

Everything was coming together. Just the way God wanted it. For Elijah.

And for you. In Gilead.

Thinking back again to some of those situations and experiences God has taken you through, how would you be less committed today, have less clarity on your purpose, or be less assured in adversity if those occurrences had not been part of your past, of your preparation, of your process? What would you lack if you hadn't experienced them?

"It is good for me that I was afflicted, that I may learn Your statutes. The law of Your mouth is better to me than thousands of gold and silver pieces. Your hands made me and fashioned me; give me understanding, that I may learn Your commandments."

PSALM 119:71-73

During Elijah's unrecorded years in Gilead, he somehow came to know, to *really* know, Yahweh. Maybe it was his father or mother who taught him the record of God's faithfulness to Israel. Maybe some of the older shepherds he worked around were in the habit of pointing out God's living, active, moving presence among them in Gilead. Maybe it was in the quietness of performing his everyday shepherding tasks that Elijah sensed God supernaturally revealing Himself to His soon-to-be representative.

One way or another, while doing his tedious, mundane, lonesome work, while facing hardships we'll never know, Elijah had been exposed to influences that convinced him Jehovah wasn't just one deity among many other options. He'd developed a deep knowledge, reverence, and understanding for Yahweh's covenant with His people, a holy perspective that would form the basis for his first prophetic declaration in Scripture. This God, Israel's God, was a jealous God who had no intention of sharing His glory with man-made idols.

That's what Elijah learned in Gilead.

- *In Gilead,* where he was from.

- *In Gilead,* where his heart was formed.

- *In Gilead,* where his own personal set of trials and difficulties became the start of a process, a process of living and thinking and navigating his journey by faith.

The backside of that raw, rugged desert was God's way of bringing Elijah around to know Him in a way he would never have experienced Him otherwise. Now he was ready to declare God's word with boldness and authority.

Elijah's whole life was about to become a clear, bold declaration of God's power and provision.

And so is yours. Where you have come from. What you have been through.

All of it has been preparing you for the purpose He's planned next for you.

As you close today's lesson, take a few moments to thank the Lord for your journey this far. Ask Him to give you the courage to trust that He is using every part of it—even the difficult or despairing parts—to form you into His image, to focus your passions and pursuits, and to funnel you into the stream of His purposes for this generation, for future generations.

ELIJAH CALLING

"Before I formed you in the womb I knew you,
and before you were born I consecrated you;
I have appointed you a prophet to the nations."

JEREMIAH 1:5

There's a beautiful woman who works in our ministry office whose first name is hardly a common one. In fact, she's spent her whole life having to both spell it and pronounce it for people, because it actually sounds nothing like the way you'd expect.

Her name is Abisha (pronounced, ah-BAH-sha). I know, right? Who'd ever guess?

Nobody, that's who.

Abisha's parents didn't give her that name just because they liked the ring of it. They wanted their daughter to be called by a name that spoke to her identity and the character they hoped she would pattern her life after. The Hebrew meaning of *Abisha* is "The Lord is my Father." It's like a banner stretched across her lifelong commitment and confession, declaring "who she is" and "who she belongs to."

I love names like that.

Because names matter.

In biblical days, names were quite often synonymous with a person's calling and character. They weren't simply nomenclature. They signified one's reputation. The syllables of Hebrew names, like a puzzle meticulously fitted together, built layer upon layer of insight into who this person really was or was meant to be. So when Elijah first arrived in town, anyone in the vicinity would have known where his allegiance stood, simply by hearing his name.

- *El,* meaning, "God"

- *I,* meaning, "my"

- *Jah,* meaning, "Yahweh"

People who knew Elijah knew where he stood, even before they really knew him.

> Consider each component of Elijah's name. Below, write what you would've inferred about his reputation and allegiance if you'd been in King Ahab's court on the day Elijah arrived there.

Yahweh is the name God calls Himself. In Hebrew tradition, His name was considered too holy even to speak aloud. So in the Old Testament, where this name appears more than six thousand times, it was changed to the word *Adonai,* which in English versions is printed as "LORD," in all capital letters.[3]

Elijah's first words to Ahab in 1 Kings 17:1 were sort of a pledge of allegiance, which corresponded with the meaning of his name. Turn to this verse and notice the layers:

- The LORD
- The LORD is _____
- The LORD is God of _____
- The LORD God of Israel _____
- The LORD God of Israel lives, and I have pledged my sole allegiance to Him.

What did Elijah say was God's impending judgment on the nation of Israel because of her rebellion?

See "Digging Deeper I" article on page 44.

Remember James 5:17? What had Elijah been doing in the weeks, possibly years leading up to this announcement?

What does this observation tell you about how Elijah viewed:

- God?

- God's Word?

- The effectiveness of prayer?

Turn to and read Deuteronomy 29, particularly verses 16-29, where God revealed the cost to be paid by those who rejected His covenant.

Based on what Elijah knew about God's covenant with His people (Deut. 29, for example), he knew Israel's duplicity necessitated judgment. But that's not all he knew. See if this doesn't blow your mind. Despite the fact that these negative results of the people's disobedience would adversely affect Elijah too—such as the land being "unsown and unproductive" so that "no grass grows in it" (Deut. 29:23)—he was brave enough and committed to God enough that he still prayed for it. Out there in Gilead, in the remote starting point of Elijah's ministry—the starting point of his process—he had developed such a commitment to Yahweh that he was willing to pray for His will to be done above all else, even above his own comfort.

And he was willing to speak this unbending truth to the most powerful man in the nation.

To whom did Elijah declare God's forthcoming judgment?

What in the world gave this uncouth, uncivilized, underdressed man from the dusty backwoods of a small town the idea that he could stand in front of a king? An unkind king, clad in fine purple robes. A jaded king, seated on a bejeweled throne. An evil king, surrounded by armed soldiers who had no respect for Yahweh's Word.

How did this guy get in here?

The answer to this question is, we don't know. Frustrating, huh? Scholars are unsure how Elijah ever ended up being granted an audience with King Ahab and why his life was spared when he did, especially considering the unwelcome message he came to deliver. Nothing other than the sovereignty of Almighty God could be responsible for arranging this unimaginable appointment.

But we do know this: they understood what this meeting was about, even before the prophet opened his mouth. Elijah's name had become synonymous with his character. His God was Yahweh.

Apparently his whole life had been shaped by the meaning of his name.

Elijah's holy passion hadn't happened overnight. And based on what we know of the spiritual decline around him, it surely hadn't happened by osmosis. But Elijah's allegiance to the Lord had become more secure with each passing day, week, and year. Long before he stood up in front of a king at court, he had spent his quiet, obscure life building the character, establishing the reputation, and securing the allegiance that reflected this reality.

So as 1 Kings 17 opens, Elijah was physically standing before a king. But his real standing—his true allegiance—was before Yahweh.

Compare and contrast these two portions of Scripture:

- Turn to John 12:42-43. How would you describe the allegiance of the Jewish leaders here? Where did they choose to stand?

- Now turn to 1 Thessalonians 2:4. How would you describe the apostle Paul's allegiance? Where did he choose to stand?

Now consider your own stance in light of these two scenarios. In what types of situations have you had your own allegiances put to the test? Where have *you* chosen to stand?

Here's another way to think about it. You are a citizen of the country in which you live. If you've traveled internationally, you've crossed borders into other nations, possibly into other continents. You've immersed yourself into different traditions and cultures in foreign regions of the world. But even when you've stood on foreign soil, your allegiance was still pledged to your country. No matter where in the world you've been privileged enough to go, your loyalty and citizenship is still secured and settled. You might have been physically standing *there*, but your standing was still *here*.

Frame your whole life like this. You can stand at that office, or attend school at that university, or participate in that organization, or answer to that supervisor, and at the same time keep your ultimate allegiance securely situated in the one true God. In fact, you *must* treat your allegiance like this if you genuinely want to honor Him. You can be standing *there*, but really be standing here, with your hand over your heart before your true Lord and King.

Because when you know your name, even if you're from a nowhere place like Gilead—when you've committed yourself to the process of learning who you are, based on the truth of the One who has called you to serve and follow Him—you can stand and declare His Word in any place, in front of anybody. You can know, like Elijah did, that your God is Yahweh, that you represent the One whom no man or worldly idol can replace, remove, or redact.

As daughter of a King, your name has been imbued with all the rights and privileges that give you access through Christ to your Father's power. Everything God has allowed you to march through in life so far has been intended to mature your faith, fortify your principles, shape your character, and cement your allegiance to Him. It's been preparing you to take your stand in that confidence.

Life is truly a process of growing into your faith, or as Peter said, growing "in the grace and knowledge of our Lord and Savior Jesus Christ" (2 Pet. 3:18). But your identity as a believer is something you wear today. Right now. *Here* is where you stand.

> Turn to 1 Peter 2:9-10 as we prepare to close this week of study. Fill in the blanks with what the Bible asserts to be your identity as a believer in Christ.

- **chosen:** you are "a chosen _____"
- **royal:** you are "a royal _____"
- **holy:** you are "a holy _____"
- **child of God:** you are God's own "_____"
- **proclaimer:** made to proclaim or declare His "_____"
- **called:** you've been called "out of _____"
- **light:** called into His marvelous, wonderful "_____"

This is who you are. Each one of these features—and more—is part of your given name. It's been your name from the moment you put faith in Christ as Savior, and it will be your name for as long as you live.

Knowing your name—knowing who you are—gives you the courage to stand on the bedrock of eternal truth, to stand there in the name of the One who "called you for a righteous purpose" (Isa. 42:6, CSB).

So when Elijah set out from Gilead, tromping out of the hills toward the city, toward the throne room of Ahab, with God's Word in his mouth and God's strength pulsating in his heart, he may not have known much. But he did know what his name meant. And there he would take his stand.

Can't wait to see in the next six weeks where it takes him. And us.

HEAVEN'S RAIN

Centuries before Elijah's prophetic ministry, Yahweh delivered the Hebrew children from brutal slavery in Egypt. As Moses led them toward Canaan, he took great care to point out an interesting contrast between the two locations. Egypt was "where you used to sow your seed and water it . . . But the land into which you are about to cross to possess it" is a land that "drinks water from the rain of heaven" (Deut. 11:10-11).

The distinction between the land of their captivity and the promised land is that the first had been irrigated by hand, but the other would be sustained and watered by the loving and faithful hand of their Deliverer. In other words, an open heaven was a sign of God's favor and blessing on His people as they continued to submit to His authority and worship Him alone.

They were warned, as they contemplated their future in Canaan:

"Beware that your hearts are not deceived, and that you do not turn away and serve other gods and worship them. Or the anger of the LORD will be kindled against you, and He will shut up the heavens so that there will be no rain and the ground will not yield its fruit; and you will perish quickly from the good land which the LORD is giving you."
DEUTERONOMY 11:16-17

This is why Elijah's pronouncement of drought to King Ahab and the nation had ramifications that went beyond a simple weather forecast. It signified the judgment of Yahweh upon Israel for their rebellion and their ongoing refusal to submit to His authority. Elijah's declaration was not rooted in his own conjecture. He knew the Word of his God, and he based his message to Ahab on the holy covenant that had been established in the wilderness.

But that's not the only thing Elijah had in mind as he prophesied the coming drought. Baal and his female cohort Asherah were recognized and worshiped as the god and goddess of fertility. It was believed that Baal also had power over rain. Storms, they thought, were in his control. So as idol worship became more widely sanctioned and practiced in Israel, then officially legislated under Ahab and Jezebel's leadership, God's people essentially rejected Yahweh as their primary source of provision. Israel increasingly believed that these false gods controlled the weather, the change of seasons, and, by extension, their crops' ability to yield a bountiful harvest. They began to believe that their ability to survive rested squarely in Baal's hands. The people appealed endlessly to the gods in hopes of garnering favor, thinking it ensured rain for their crops and continued productivity in their agrarian society.

Each month the sky withheld rain was an unmitigated personal strike against the authority of Baal to control nature. As an impotent idol, he had no control whatsoever over the rain and sun. Each of the one thousand, two hundred-plus days of drought and famine would remind the people that only one God held supreme authority, and their allegiance should be to Him only.

The judgments God exacted on ancient Israel are a reminder to us that any consequences we endure today are never about the consequences alone. They are designed to underscore the impotence of our idols, debunk the myth of their power, and remind us that God alone is worthy of our loyalty and worship. Whenever we anchor our significance unwisely,

putting our trust in health, success, material wealth, or relationships, thereby turning them into illegitimate gods, our Father will cut them off at the knees and remind us of their insufficiency to save.

"Like scarecrows in a cucumber patch, their idols cannot speak. They must be carried because they cannot walk. Do not fear them for they can do no harm—and they cannot do any good. LORD, there is no one like you. You are great; your name is great in power."
JEREMIAH 10:5-6, CSB

Cherith

THE PART NOBODY SEES

WEEK TWO

PREPARATION BY SEPARATION

THE PREPARATION PROCESS

1. God wants to _____ you.

Here's how you know when God is beginning to _____ you for the next season in your journey with Him. He calls you to _____ your grasp on something, someone, or someplace.

Ask the Holy Spirit to spotlight any specific ways where God is asking you to _____ _____ from here, to get up and get out, to relocate and _____ your life in some way.

2. God wants to _____ you.

Give God the opportunity to show you what it's like to be _____ by God and God _____.

Open your eyes to see the water He has given you in that place where it's _____ or might feel _____ to you.

3. God wants to _____ you.

According to Ephesians 3:20-21, God does exceedingly, abundantly, above and beyond anything that you can _____ or _____.

4. God wants to _____ you.

Elijah had no idea that while he was being obedient in _____, he was actually being _____ from something he didn't even know he was in danger of.

Video and audio sessions available for purchase
and rent at LifeWay.com/Elijah.

SEPARATION ANXIETY

"Go, my people, enter your rooms and close your doors behind you. Hide for a little while until the wrath has passed."

ISAIAH 26:20, CSB

Before the year 2020, most of us had never heard the phrase "social distancing." Then within what seemed like a matter of days, we went from meeting with friends at local coffee shops to wearing face masks, quarantining in our homes, and using technology as our only means of interaction. Sequester? Quarantine? Suddenly these concepts were not just for political prisoners, poison victims, and criminal juries anymore. They were for all of us.

Turns out though, this idea of setting oneself apart has long been part of God's process in developing His people for usefulness and impact. Jesus demonstrated it Himself, enduring forty days of solitude before entering into public ministry (Matt. 4:1). Throughout His earthly life, He would often "slip away to the wilderness" (Luke 5:16) to be alone with God, usually "in the early morning, while it was still dark" (Mark 1:35). Socially distant—before the rest of us even knew social distance was a thing.

As far back as 1 Kings 17, we see Yahweh prescribe for Elijah a season of separation as a necessary stop on the prophet's journey to spiritual maturity and victory.

> "Go away from here and turn eastward, and hide yourself by the brook Cherith, which is east of the Jordan."
>
> **1 KINGS 17:3**

Turn to 1 Kings 17:2-4 in your Bible. Focusing on verse 3 in the margin, what are the three actions that God required Elijah to take.

1.

2.

3.

ELIJAH

As you begin this week of study, ask the Holy Spirit to give you clarity in responding to the following three related questions:

1. In what area of life have you sensed God asking you to *leave* or *go away from* anything or anyone that's been a customary part of how you operate?

2. What direction have you felt the Spirit *turning* you toward?

3. What will it require for you to fully *hide yourself* and completely engage in this new location if you're to receive every bit of development He's planned for you in this space and season?

Oh, and one final question. Important: Have you complied with the Spirit's conviction in these matters? If not, what do you think has kept you from it?

While Cherith's precise GPS coordinates remain a mystery to modern explorers, its dynamics do not. All the land "east of the Jordan" was rugged and unkempt. Dotted with a variety of mountains and hills, its valleys were as deep as its peaks were high. It was known for its long stretches of lonely wasteland, broken only by thin streams of trickling water here and there, like the brook called simply, singularly, *Cherith*.

Cherith is a place name meaning "cutting" or "ditch."[1]

No one now knows for sure where this narrow stream (pronounced KEER-ith) was located. But Elijah knew. Concealed in the hills, this rivulet where God had called him to sequester himself was a place of pervasive silence and widespread solitude. This secluded spot away from everything was the perfect place for God to accomplish the next stage of His intended work in the life of His servant.

Consider some of the dynamics Elijah would be leaving behind—within the palace, for example, where he'd just begun his public ministry as a prophet of Yahweh—and the stark contrast Cherith presented him. Write some of your observations below.

"The [one] who is to take a high place before his fellows must take a low place before his God, and there is no better manner of bringing a man down than by suddenly dropping him out of a sphere to which he was beginning to think himself essential, teaching him that he is not at all necessary to God's plan and compelling him to consider in the sequestered vale of some Cherith how [imbalanced] are his motives and how insignificant his strength."[2]
—F. B. Meyer

The bustling activities and polished accoutrements that characterized life at the center of the action were a far cry from where Elijah was going. Stones and scorpions were more ubiquitous around Cherith than people and luxuries. But Elijah's calling for the time being would not keep him in proximity of the palace or amid the throbbing heart of the masses, where he could see up-close the effect of his drought pronouncement on the king and his people. Instead he was being ordered to sequester himself, out where he'd not be able to consult with or depend on any other human, to simply be alone with his God. Here he'd need to entrust the results of his ministry to the One who'd called him to Ahab's court in the first place, and who just as clearly had called him away now into the next leg of the process.

F. B. Meyer is one of my favorite theologians. You'll find a quote from him in the margin regarding Elijah's time at Cherith. Read it over, and then meet me back here to consider a few of its choice nuggets.

- "Suddenly dropping him out of a sphere": When God "suddenly" removes us from a season that's been populated with many people and relationships into one that's marked by solitude, it can be unsettling. Why might such an abrupt shift sometimes be necessary in adjusting our perspectives, pruning our pride, and reorienting our priorities?

- "Beginning to think himself essential": It's easy to feel as if we're "essential" to God's work getting done. We can begin to carry a weight that is His alone to bear, then expect the glory that is His alone to receive. How might Cherith realign this thinking in Elijah and in us?

- "How imbalanced are his motives": Often we can't see our inner selves clearly until we get quiet, without the distractions of a full and hectic life. How can the "sequestered vale of some Cherith" help bring these discrepancies of motive into sharper view?

Mind if I just speak to you from my own heart and experience for a second? Everybody's life is different; I understand that. But as I look back on mine, I see where at every turn, every time God has been preparing me to tackle a fresh challenge or to move into a new spiritual place with Him, the process He's chosen has almost always begun with a stop in "Cherith"—a season of life that I perceived at the time to be undesirably obscure, isolating, unproductive, and relatively mundane.

Truth be told, I haven't always complied quickly or easily with wherever God was sending me—at least not voluntarily, as Elijah appeared to do. God has often needed to push me, closing doors in one direction, lighting my path to another, severing and resetting relationships, then diverting me toward Cherith and the disciplines and values He knew it would develop in me: a renewed passion for prayer, a fresh hunger for His voice, and a clearer focus on His priorities.

Finally upon coming to my "Cherith," I've often struggled there through a sense of loneliness and insecurity, of being unseen. I haven't always understood why this stage of the process is necessary. It's sometimes seemed to me like a waste of weeks, months, and years, away from the work He's been calling me to do—work that seems a lot more important to me than the little I appeared to be accomplishing while at Cherith. But just as Elijah apparently needed to learn, I'm not as necessary to the greater work of God, as much as the greater work of God is necessary in me.

The "sequestered vale" of Cherith is where He keeps teaching me this. And whenever He's wanted to reshape and refocus me in areas where my flesh has begun to take control, or just to prepare me for the next stage of my journey with Him, He whispers:

> *Priscilla, My daughter, trust Me. Go away from where you've been. Cut unnecessary strings to passions, ambitions, people, and pleasures that are dividing your affections and allegiance. Turn your energy and attention in a new direction, toward new goals that I will show you. Hide yourself there, and rest until I release you.*

Pay attention when you sense God's Spirit speaking to you in this way. Notice they're the same three things He said to Elijah:

1. **"GO AWAY FROM HERE."** When the Spirit begins to whisper this directive, you'll sense a rise of conviction in your soul about a current aspect of your life, compelling you to leave behind a habit, an ambition, perhaps even a relationship you may not want to leave. (I'm not talking about God-honoring commitments you've made to your spouse or children, of course, but entanglements with certain people that are keeping you from going where He wants you to go.)

2. **"TURN."** As you obey and separate yourself, He'll begin to show you a new direction, interest, or goal to pivot toward. This clarity might not be immediate, but He will slowly begin reorienting your heart and hands in a new direction. When He does, go that way. *Turn* that way.

3. **"HIDE."** Fully immerse yourself in the lessons He wants to teach you and the spiritual disciplines He longs to renew in you. Fully divest yourself from the idols pulling back against your commitment to Him and making you halfhearted. Then press into the new internal postures and external dynamics that Cherith requires. Rest here until He determines it's time to release you.

In thinking about these three steps, do you currently see the Lord dealing with you in any specific way? If so, which one? Which step? Which aspects of your relationship with Him point to this?

Take a look at how this process of *separation* helped shape the lives of well-known biblical personalities:

Choose any two of the following biblical case studies:

- Joseph (Gen. 39:11-23)
- Moses (Ex. 2:11-12)
- Samuel (1 Sam. 1:20-28)
- Paul (Gal. 1:15-24)

For each, consider the following questions:

- Where did they end up going or being sent that may have seemed unnecessary or even adverse to their ultimate goals?

- What indicates God's hand was still on them while they were there?

- How did God bring good to them in those places?

- Knowing what you know of their futures, how might these seasons of separation have been essential to God's purposes for them?

Joseph didn't yet know, while in prison, that his character was being shaped for becoming the compassionate prime minister of Egypt. *Moses*, in the fields of Midian, far away from his people, could never have imagined he'd be commissioned as Israel's lead freedom fighter. *Samuel*, separated as a child from his parents, didn't know his future service would require an ear for God's voice that needed the quietness of God's house as a learning laboratory. *Paul* didn't know his years in obscurity were preparing him to be one of the primary apostles of the first-century church.

Isolation proved vital in God's process of preparing them for lives of maximum fruitfulness. It's where their passions were shaped and their ambitions were purified, where they met God in new and unexpected ways.

Their missions, their ministries, were each mammoth in scope. But in each case, the mettle they needed for it was forged in places far away from where God ultimately took them. Periods of seclusion did not devalue or derail them or denote a lapse in God's pleasure toward them. Instead, as with Elijah, isolation proved vital in God's process of preparing them for lives of maximum fruitfulness. It's where their passions were shaped and their ambitions were purified, where they met God in new and unexpected ways.

Elijah, unbeknownst to him, was being prepared for a public showdown that would demand a level of courage, conviction, and inner fortitude he did not yet possess. And Cherith was one of the places where God would produce it in him.

Don't despise the sequestered solitude of Cherith, sister. The spiritual power you desire (and will soon require) cannot be cultivated any other place.

MY PROVIDER

"You will drink of the brook . . ."

1 KINGS 17:4, NASB

When my boys were younger, we'd often take walks behind one of my best friend's houses, crossing her back acreage until we came to a thick cove of trees. Once past the timberline, we felt as though we'd entered another world. We'd look for large branches to use as walking sticks, then pretend we were exploring a giant forest with no other inhabitants in sight.

Few things are much more naturally adventurous than trekking through the woods with three little boys, climbing over rocks, balancing yourself on fallen trees, listening for sounds, looking for bugs. But most of all, we enjoyed the part of the property where a small brook ran through. Sometimes after a heavy rain, it would be filled with water that danced around the rocks, rushing downstream where it emptied into a larger creek. At other times though, particularly in summer, when rain in Texas plays hard to get, the stream bed would be as dry as a cotton ball.

That's the thing about brooks. They aren't consistent. You can't count on them. Brooks are sometime-y. If it doesn't rain, they don't hold any water.

That's the thing about Cherith too. It was just a little unreliable brook. A brook that needed rain in order to thrive. And the rain, as you know, was ending. God had told Elijah to say there'd be "neither dew nor rain" in these parts for a number of years (1 Kings 17:1). So the effect on this brook and its lone inhabitant was inescapable. What would happen after Elijah had been at Cherith for more than a few days? Without rain?

> Think of several dynamics in your life right now (work, people, health, financial prospects, etc.) that have proven unreliable because of their lack of consistency. Write down the first two examples that come to mind.

Is there any way in which you've resented God or questioned His kindness toward you for sending you to this "Cherith," knowing its limitations?

Some versions of 1 Kings 17:4 may use the word *wadi,* the Hebrew term for "brook." Wadis, which are numerous in the Middle East, are rocky watercourses that are dry except for rainy seasons.[3]

Elijah had been raised in this neck of the woods and knew about brooks like Cherith, just like my boys and I knew about the brook not far from our backyard. He knew it came with serious limitations as a water source, particularly during a time of national drought.

That's what makes Elijah's yielded obedience to God's instruction about hiding himself at Cherith even more astounding. He obeyed even with this risky reality in mind. Surrendering to Yahweh's assignment would've been more understandable if God had told him to go hang out beside a *river*. A river could resist the effects of drought much longer. But the combination of famine and a fickle brook, along with God's directive to go hide there for an extended period of time, must have sounded like a really bad idea. And yet the prophet obeyed.

I believe his unreserved obedience was primarily prompted by one thing:

Read 1 Kings 17:3-4a, printed below. Circle God's promise to Elijah.

"Go away from here and turn eastward, and hide yourself by the brook Cherith, which is east of the Jordan. It shall be that you will drink of the brook [wadi] . . ."

Now write this promise verbatim below.

Just so you know, I've repeated this promise throughout your entire devotional today. It's at the top of today's lesson, and you'll see it again and again. My hope is that its truth will nestle deeply inside your soul, quieting any anxiety you may feel about your next experience at Cherith and filling you with a sense of peace about it when it comes.

Sister, don't skim over the spectacular revelation to be gleaned from just this tiny sliver of Scripture. God intentionally hid His beloved prophet near a water source that was at best seasonal. In fact, we'll notice it soon enough in our study next week. When God was ready to move Elijah on to his next part of the process, this *wadi* did what *wadis* do. It dried up.

God in His sovereignty knew this would happen. *Before He sent him.* Yet throughout the entire time that Elijah obediently hid there, surrendering to a season of seclusion and training, of waiting and hiding, God told Elijah not to worry about where his water would come from. The God of oceans made him a promise: "You will drink of the brook." You will.

Your needs will be met. You will be refreshed. No question. No matter. No ifs, ands, or buts.

Pause and absorb this truth for a moment. Your new *position* at Cherith has come with a *promise*. A promise of God's care and provision. Thank Him for this, even while perhaps you sit there today beside a brook in your own life that's looking mighty dry right now.

In the margin, write how you intend to change your attitude, approach, and actions regarding the undependable dynamics in your life, in light of the following promises:

- "I will never desert you, nor will I ever forsake you" (Heb. 13:5).

- "The Lord will rescue me from every evil attack and will bring me safely to his heavenly kingdom" (2 Tim. 4:18a, NIV).

- "God is able to make all grace abound to you, so that always having all sufficiency in everything, you may have an abundance for every good deed" (2 Cor. 9:8).

- "If we ask anything according to His will, He hears us" (1 John 5:14b).

- "If any of you lacks wisdom, let him ask of God, who gives to all generously and without reproach, and it will be given to him" (Jas. 1:5).

- "Sustain me as you promised, and I will live; do not let me be ashamed of my hope. Sustain me so that I can be safe and always be concerned about your statutes" (Ps. 119:116-117, CSB).

These are just a few of the promises that give you confidence, like Elijah, to yield to God's work at your Cherith when you see it beginning to run dry. The unpredictable people and circumstances in your life will not be able to unsettle you nearly as much when you're resting in God's Word that says, "Even to your old age and gray hairs I am he, I am he who will sustain you. I have made you and I will carry you; I will sustain you and I will rescue you" (Isa. 46:4, NIV). Your peace and provision are not rooted in the undependable things around you. Your hope is embedded in something else. In Someone else.

"You will drink of the brook."

That's a promise.

"God is not a man, that he might lie, or a son of man, that he might change his mind. Does he speak and not act, or promise and not fulfill?"

NUMBERS 23:19, CSB

← Read Numbers 23:19 in the margin, underlining some of the key words and phrases that stand out to you as being most encouraging. How does God's nature and His promise compare with the lack of reliability you've often experienced from other things and other people in your life?

God will provide. God will supply. When you're going through times of *separation* from your usual surroundings, remember you are not separated from the One who's promised to sustain you where He's placed you. Your available resources may feel shaky and uncertain, but if He sent you there, then He will sustain you there. He will not fail to "supply all your needs according to His riches in glory in Christ Jesus" (Phil. 4:19).

That's a Cherith provision promise.

Yahweh's promise—"You will drink of the brook"—was designed to teach Elijah the same lesson your fickle Cherith is intended to teach you—a truth that Elijah would need to know without any doubt before he ever stepped foot on Mount Carmel. His real source of sustenance was not the inadequate resources of the brook Cherith, any more than if it had been the vast, robust waters of the Mediterranean Sea. The ultimate source of Elijah's provision was God Himself.

Underline the last line of the previous paragraph. Then fill in the blanks of the two statements below:

• God is reminding me that my _____ source of _____ is Him.

• God is teaching me not to anchor my trust in _____
_____
_____
_____
_____.

(Personalize your answer to your own circumstances. Feel free to enumerate them all over the page, all the way out to the edge.)

Yahweh allows the stuff of Earth to be lacking in its ability to fulfill us so that we have no choice but to look to Him for our ultimate satisfaction.

My ultimate source of provision is God Himself.

#ElijahBibleStudy

• When you are lonely, God is your friend.
• When you are tired, God is your strength.
• When you are hungry, _____ is your Bread of life.
• When you are dry, _____ is your Living Water.
• When you are insecure, _____ is your confidence.
• When you are empty, _____ is your fulfillment.

If God has placed you alongside a brook *like this*, in a dry season *like this*—a wadi that hasn't been reliable in providing what you need, whether relationally or financially or physically or emotionally—hear God's Word to you again and let it give you strength and security.

"You will drink of the brook."

If only you will look to your Father, remember His promises, and live in light of their assurances, you will not die from thirst while you're waiting with God in Cherith. Despite the disappointment, frustration, and real concern you may be feeling, "Don't worry about anything; instead, pray about everything" (Phil. 4:6, NLT). Because when He alone is your source, you can rest and be at ease despite the drying brook before you, behind you, or beside you. Your inner life can be nourished, pulsing with a peace that blossoms from His promises.

SOMEWHERE IN-BETWEEN

"If they had been thinking of that country from which they went out, they would have had opportunity to return. But as it is, they desire a better country."

HEBREWS 11:15-16

Joshua, my friend Shawna's older son, as I shared with you last week, is a cadet at West Point, the United States Military Academy. I've known him since the day he was born, which makes it even harder for me to believe how he's suddenly become a grown man. Not that he wasn't already strong and mature for his age, but he's different now. West Point has made him different. Being a young Army cadet has shaved off whatever remained of any teenage recklessness and frivolity, replacing it with the meaty stuff of refined manhood: the visible bearing of self-discipline, respect and submission to authority, and honor for himself and for others around him.

It started in boot camp. First-year cadets—*plebes*, as the upperclassmen (not so lovingly) call them—arrive on campus with few freedoms. The rigid routine of their all-day, all-night schedule is harsh and unforgiving. Every single area of their lives is regulated. Unlike freshmen in other colleges, who can trot home every weekend for mama's cooking and laundry services, the rules regarding *plebes* restrict their family visits to a total of eight specific days for the entire two semesters, none of which exceed a strict 24–48 hours in duration.

That's just the military way. In order to be instilled with the mind-sets, attitudes, priorities, and behaviors that will make them ready to discharge their duties in any situation, they need a clean, intentional distance from the life they were accustomed to living before entering the academy.

They need to resist the urge to go home.

Turn to and read Exodus 15:27–16:3. You're catching the children of Israel after they'd been delivered from Egypt, after they'd been chased by Pharaoh's army, and after they'd escaped through the Red Sea. Write the place name in verse 27 that tells where they'd reached. What was it like?

According to Exodus 16:1, what was their location? This place was "between" Elim and where?

How does verse 2 describe this in-between place? How did the Israelites feel about being there? What did they do "against Moses and Aaron"?

Verse 3. How would you paraphrase the people's complaint about their current situation?

They wished they were back home, even if *home* to them was altogether incompatible with the plan and purpose God had claimed on their lives. Or they wished they were going forward. And going there faster. They wanted to hurry on to Sinai where Moses said he'd met with God face-to-face, where the Lord had said to him, "When you have brought the people out of Egypt, you shall worship God at this mountain" (Ex. 3:12).

But from the middle of a dry, barren wilderness, all they could seem to think about were the dinner plates and aromas from the only home they'd ever known. They thought of it even more strongly than the prospect of being up-close and personal with God or of moving on from there to the "land flowing with milk and honey" that they'd been told was in their future (Ex. 13:5b).

They'd rather go back than go forward or rather go forward than just sit. The worst place of all, they believed, was being stuck there *in-between*.

Now let's look again at 1 Kings 17:2-5. I realize we've been in this passage for an extended stay, but I love studying the Bible this way. Bit by bit, line by line. Looking again at verse 3, what was the repeated geographical emphasis that was part of God's instructions to Elijah? In which direction did Yahweh want him to head?

Now flip back to the map located on the inside back cover of your book.

• First, circle *Samaria*. This is where Elijah met with Ahab in verse 1, where he was currently located.

• Second, circle *Tishbe*. This, you'll recall, is where Elijah was born and raised.

• Third, find the *Jordan River*. God had told him to go just east of there to Cherith.

Consider the geographical position of these places. How would you summarize Elijah's positioning and his potential dilemma?

Elijah had been dead set on going to the palace, based on what his prophetic ears had picked up as God's immediate instructions concerning Ahab, Israel, and the coming drought. Yahweh's calling on his life had brought him out of his element and away from the comforts and familiarity of his home, down from the mountain passes and onto the road that led toward Samaria, capital city of the Northern Kingdom. Here is where he delivered his one-sentence, long-range forecast to the nation's ruler, making everyone uncomfortable, agitating Samaria's inhabitants with his prophetic declaration.

Then God told him to go back. Back east, toward home. But not *to* it.

Cherith was the in-between.

> When was the last time you longed impatiently for home—
> to go back to the comfort and familiarity of a previous
> season of life that God clearly called you away from?

> What are the easy-feeling, easygoing allures of home
> that most frequently tempt you away from the places and
> expectations that God's Spirit is leading you to press into?

> What difficulties or doubts about your current
> circumstances escalate this desire?

The comfort zone of home life can often be just as damaging to our spiritual growth as the enticing attraction of future ambition. That's why sometimes, in order to get us adequately prepared for the moments to come, God may not allow us to return to the way things used to be, the place where we could easily become lulled into complacency. When God needs us bold and fervent and clear of mind—when He wants our faith primed and pregnant for His fire to fall—He'll often call us to an in-between place. Not quite where we're going to be, but not all the way back where we were.

Elijah's wadi was *in-between* Samaria and Gilead. Not quite there, not quite here. Neither the center of the action, nor the sweet spot of the sofa.

That's when you know you're in Cherith—when you feel like you're languishing between the unrealized fruition of well-meaning ambitions and the formerly fine habits and habitats of a former season of your life—when neither one feels open to you with a clear conscience and

Sometimes, in order to get us adequately prepared for the moments to come, God may not allow us to return to the way things used to be, the place where we could easily become lulled into complacency.

#ElijahBibleStudy

an assurance of God's leading. In times like these, you'll need to resist two distinct urges: (1) the temptation to barrel ahead and push the doors of Samaria open yourself in an effort to force God's timing, and (2) the appeal to run back home, where you know there's respite in the form of sameness and settled surroundings. People you've grown to love. Things you're accustomed to doing. Patterns of behavior that fit around your heart like a fleecy sweatshirt.

In order to prepare for Carmel, God sent Elijah not as far east as Elijah might have preferred to go. But if he hadn't listened and obeyed his Lord, if he'd scurried on home anyway, its comforts could have fostered complacency. And complacency could have robbed him of the character required for Carmel. He wouldn't have had the confidence in God, the trust in God's provision, that he learned by experience at the shallow, inadequate, in-between brook called Cherith.

And neither will we. Neither will you.

The inadequacy of your Cherith is fortifying a holy courage and confidence you'll need for later. Don't shortcut the process.

> Hebrews 11 (the so-called Hall of Faith) tells of men and women throughout biblical history who were willing to stay in-between with God despite natural desires that called them elsewhere. They were "looking forward to the city that has foundations, whose architect and builder is God" (v. 10). Choose one of the following people to see what you can learn from their experience.
>
> • Noah (v. 7)
> • Abraham (vv. 8-10)
> • Moses (vv. 23-29)
>
> What did God call this person to do?

How would going home (or staying home) have changed his future?

What did God enable him to accomplish through trust and faith?

My friend's son Joshua is making a fine soldier. He's becoming more of a man, able to endure tougher challenges and impossible situations than he likely ever dreamed himself capable of doing. Staying home would be nice. Even visiting there on a more frequent basis during college would feel like a real blessing to him (and his mom!). But the courage required to be a military officer who is equipped and readied for the future cannot be curated in the cozy comforts of his childhood home.

Life in the middle can be unsettling, but don't be discouraged. Stay put. Trust God, and in due time He'll move you on.

DAY FOUR

SURPRISE, SURPRISE

"I have commanded the ravens to provide for you there."

1 KINGS 17:4b

One of my favorite portions of Scripture is found at the end of the third chapter of Ephesians. The apostle Paul concluded the first half of his letter to the church at Ephesus with two verses that form one of the most spectacular doxologies in the whole New Testament.

> "Now to Him who is able to do exceedingly abundantly above all that we ask or think, according to the power that works in us, to Him be glory in the church by Christ Jesus to all generations, forever and ever. Amen."

EPHESIANS 3:20-21, NKJV

Breathtaking, isn't it? Read those two verses again, and circle any words or phrases that resonate with you right now in your life. Below, articulate why you find them so meaningful.

The part of Paul's praise song that makes my heart bubble with holy, excited anticipation is not only that God is able to accomplish things beyond my capacity to verbalize them in prayer (beyond what I can "ask"), but also that He can craft solutions and remedies for me beyond my ability to reason.

Beyond what I can THINK!

If you and I were blessed with the brightest minds in the world, we'd still remain limited in our thoughts about God, whether about His glory or His miraculous potential. We still wouldn't be in the same galaxy of comprehension where our omniscient, omnipresent, sovereign God operates every single day. Even when we're functioning at the highest levels of our cognitive capacities, we haven't yet reached the mere fringes of what is possible for Him to do.

ELIJAH

In other words, your loving Father has categories of answers, solutions, and options for you and your life that you don't even know exist.

They're beyond what you can think. Which, in part, is why God brought Elijah (and why His Spirit brings us) to Cherith—to show us things He can do that we would've never thought possible.

To surprise us.

Think of it. God not only intended to meet Elijah's need for water ("you will drink of the brook") but also for food—promises that were miraculous in themselves, given the isolated location of Cherith and the impending drought.

Lack of rainwater notwithstanding, Elijah knew what the geography and environs around Cherith were like. There's a good chance it lay between two perpendicular walls of mountain. The soil in that location wasn't soft and rich. It wasn't capable of producing lush, sustainable vegetation. This was dry, parched, thirsty, fallow ground. Even if he'd tried, Elijah knew he couldn't feed himself there. It was *unthinkable*.

God had put him in a position where no other options were possible—no other options than God Himself. Elijah had no choice but to trust God and God alone for His daily bread.

This is where the element of surprise showed up at Elijah's Cherith: "The ravens brought him bread and meat in the morning and bread and meat in the evening" (1 Kings 17:6).

Ravens?! Let's explore this together.

> Centuries earlier, as Noah's ark floated across the flooded landscape of Earth, he sent out a raven, and later a series of doves, in search of dry land. Read a portion of this account in Genesis 8:6-9. Compare the behaviors of the two birds. What did the raven do that the dove didn't?

Your loving Father has categories of answers, solutions, and options that you don't even know exist.

#ElijahBibleStudy

What clues does this story give you about the normal tendency of ravens?

Why might God have chosen a bird with this kind of inclination to bring meat and bread to Elijah each day, as opposed to a docile, tamer species?

People who study such things say ravens rarely if ever return to the same place day after day. They are restless by nature, not easily managed or trained. They're more famously known for their voracious appetite and insatiable greed. One author describes them as "flying garbage disposals"[4]—indiscriminate eaters who'll consume anything available, even if it's decaying flesh left unattended or stolen from other birds or animals.

We don't know exactly how long Elijah stayed at Cherith, but "some believe that it was at least a year—maybe longer."[5] If that's true, these ravens—these flocks of unsettled, unsharing, untrustworthy ravens—fed him nearly a thousand meals. I ask you: What were the odds of any bread and meat actually making it from the beaks of any kind of bird, much less *this* kind, to the breakfast and dinner table of Elijah in Cherith?

Perhaps if God had chosen doves or robins to perform this twice-daily, turn-down service, some kind of brilliant, brainiac ornithologist could come up with a scientific hypothesis, describing how birds of that type might be capable of pinpointing a singular location day after day. God, however, chose a bunch of ravens for the job, thereby dispelling all rational theories.

It's just beyond what anyone would think. Or rationalize. Or could ever completely comprehend.

Look back over your life and recall a time when God sustained you in a way that was particularly shocking. Jot down a few details that defied reason and resisted rationalization. Prepare to share this story with your group when you meet again. Your testimony will build the faith of another sister.

Cherith is designed to give us a front row seat to the unexplainable options of God, causing us to marvel sometimes not only at what He provides but how. Our experiences there translate into testimonies we tell to younger sisters coming up behind us, times when God used the most unreasonable person, or opened the most inconceivable door, or presented the most shocking opportunity or alternative or remedy in meeting our need. It never crossed our mind to pray that way. We hadn't even *thought* of it. But that's how God did it.

He did it like *that!*

I asked you to look back. Now I ask you to look directly in front of you. Think carefully about something you're asking of God today and believing Him for your tomorrow. Is there any way, knowingly or unknowingly, that you've been boxing Him into a certain method for how He'll answer you, possibly limiting your ability to see and receive the blessing God has for you? Having made your request known, have you fully trusted Him to do what He wants to do, the way He wants to do it? Chew on that a little. The passages in the margin will help. ⟶

Cherith teaches us to always leave God room for the element of surprise. He knows how to work through the most unlikely of delivery systems.

Consider a further reason why Elijah would never have thought of ravens as being an instrument God might use to care for him. Read the excerpt from Leviticus 11 on the following page (this is God talking to the early children of Israel), then record the insight you glean from it.

"You are to abhor these birds. They must not be eaten because they are abhorrent: eagles, bearded vultures, Egyptian vultures, kites, any kind of falcon, *every kind of raven*, ostriches, short-eared owls, gulls, any kind of hawk . . ."

LEVITICUS 11:13-16, CSB, *EMPHASIS MINE*

Given the historical relationship between ravens and Jews, what might your reaction have been if you were Elijah and God told you how He intended to deliver your miraculous meals?

Elijah would've been taught the dietary principles of Leviticus 11 from a young age. If his mother ever caught him with a fried raven sandwich in his lunchbox, he'd have wished he hadn't traded for it. As a careful, law-abiding Jew, he would never have wanted to eat or touch anything associated with "abhorrent" ravens. These birds were culturally, religiously unclean. Repulsive.

And yet they were God's choice for feeding Elijah? Pretty unthinkable, if you ask me.

Let's look quickly at another biblical account where this same principle of God's *unthinkable* solution came into play. In 2 Kings 5, Naaman (a Syrian military officer) went to Israel to see Elisha (Elijah's protégé) about a cure for his leprosy. Elisha told him to dip himself seven times in the Jordan River, then his degrading skin condition would be healed. This treatment option highly offended Naaman. He left in a huff. Weren't the rivers back home in Damascus "better than all the waters of Israel? Could I not wash in them and be clean?" (2 Kings 5:12). God's method was beneath him, too dirty and deplorable for Naaman to deal with.

What kinds of spiritual threads do you see woven into Naaman's refusal?

How might dealing with spiritual vices like pride, superiority, and bias have been the purpose behind how God offered to meet Elijah's need as well?

As with Naaman, God's plans are rarely if ever intended only to heal our leprosy. His intention is to heal our hearts, to *teach* us something, to *show* us things about ourselves that, if learned, can make us less narrow, prideful, and legalistic, and more open and useful for His future purposes.

Maybe a prejudicial bias needs quelling, a pedestal needs dismantling, a pocket of pride needs addressing, or, as in Elijah's case, a religious perspective needs to be progressively demolished so our hearts are ready for what's next. That's why He'll often tie the means of our provision to a vessel that bristles against our preferences. Our initial resistance or embarrassment shines a spotlight on the part that needs to be touched and sanctified for the next stage.

Maybe a root of bitterness needs unearthing, and so our solution comes from the hand of an enemy. Maybe an unhealthy habit needs breaking, and so His provision comes in a way that exposes our addictive tendency and necessitates that we deal with it. Sometimes we'd almost rather stay hungry than allow our needs to be met through such an unlikely, unthinkable conduit. But God, by surrounding us with the ravens of Cherith, teaches us to be open to the vessels He chooses.

God will provide for you as His child, yes. But He's going to do more. He's going to surprise you. And it's going to grow your faith in the process.

> Spend time in closing today with your heavenly Father, confessing any areas of resistance you feel toward His chosen ways of operating. And as you sit there, pouring out your heart to Him in honesty, surrender yourself to the freedom of receiving not only *what* He knows you really need, but also *how* He knows you really need it to arrive. Then ask Him to expose any areas of your inner life where pride or presumption needs to be replaced by humility and the tenderness of His Spirit.

SHIELDS UP

"You are my hiding place; You preserve me from trouble; You surround me with songs of deliverance."

PSALM 32:7

I'm in my mid-forties now. Not quite old enough to say I have the wisdom of my many dear mentors and elders, but far enough down the road to say I've unwrapped a gift that seems to keep on giving.

The gift of *hindsight*.

Hindsight opens a window of clarity that isn't accessible to us in real time, back when the things in question were actually happening. In the harried moment, the details and nuances were blurred and hazy. Hindsight clarifies them later into a more identifiable shape. We get it now. We wonder how we ever missed seeing it earlier. Hindsight slowly but surely answers our unanswered questions. It layers a sense of redemption and meaning across past disappointments and difficulties. It bolsters our confidence in God's ability to turn today's messes into tomorrow's message and masterpiece. Hindsight affirms what Romans 8:28 always promised, that "all things" truly do "work together for good," no matter how implausible it seemed at first.

I've asked you before to think back, to see how God brought beauty and benefits from times in your life that seemed completely incapable of it. Today I'm asking it another way: How have you looked back on those times and discovered that God, by taking you through them when He did, was actually *protecting* you—keeping you *safe* from something or someone—*shielding* you from a possible outcome you didn't even know to be guarding against?

Cherith, for Elijah, was a place like that. Looking in retrospect, through the gift of hindsight, we see that while God was *sequestering* Elijah and *sustaining* him, even *surprising* him, He was also doing something else. He was *shielding* him from dangers that Elijah didn't realize were out there. God was shielding him from challenges Elijah wasn't yet prepared to handle.

> **Let's fast-forward in Elijah's story, three years after he pronounced the judgment of famine on the land. Turn to 1 Kings 18:1-10. What did Elijah discover had been happening in Israel while he'd been hidden away at Cherith?**

Yes, while Elijah had been tucked away by the drying wadi, many others knew what Elijah was just finding out. God had been strategically, intentionally shielding him from the seething searchlight of an angry king. In 1 Kings 17, the Bible said nothing about how Ahab initially reacted to Elijah or his doomsday pronouncement. But behind the biblical scenes, as we learn in 1 Kings 18, Ahab was so outraged by Elijah's prediction that he sent a task force all over the land of Israel looking for this man he would later dub the "troubler of Israel" (1 Kings 18:17). Ahab believed Elijah was at fault for all the difficulty this drought was causing, and he wanted the prophet to pay. Maybe if Elijah was dead, Ahab reasoned, the awful famine would end.

"As the LORD your God lives, there is no nation or kingdom where my master [Ahab] has not sent to search for you; and when they said, 'He is not here,' he made the kingdom or nation swear that they could not find you."

1 KINGS 18:10

We have no indication Elijah was aware of any of this while at Cherith, or later at Zarephath (the place you and I are going next week in our study). All he knew was that "the word of the LORD came to him" (1 Kings 17:2) immediately after he left the king's presence, instructing him to head toward Cherith—dull, dry, drought-stricken Cherith— likely the last place he wanted to go. Turns out though, Cherith was actually God's secure hiding place that kept Elijah off the grid, out of radar range, where nobody would think to look for him no matter how intently they searched. Right there in the center of God's will, the prophet was supernaturally shielded so that any searchlights pointed in his direction were incapable of exposing his presence no matter how brightly they shone.

A little review from this week. In just a few words, what have been some of your biggest learnings from what God was doing when He:

• *Separated* Elijah in Cherith?

• *Sustained* Elijah in Cherith?

• *Surprised* Elijah in Cherith?

And now, come to find out, He was also *shielding* Elijah in Cherith.

Taken together, what do these observations tell you about why it's so critical that we trust God with each season of life, resisting the urge to leave Cherith prematurely out of boredom, fear, or insecurity?

I often have conversations with younger women who are carrying a number of goals and ambitions around with them, ambitions pertaining to their career or their ministry or their family life or their relationships. And they're discouraged. In their opinion, God has tucked them away on the rough, solitary, mundane soil of some "Cherith," and He's left them feeling forgotten and unfruitful. Their lives just aren't blossoming in the way they'd envisioned. Know the feeling?

This portion of Elijah's story that you and I are studying today is the one I often use to encourage them. In fact, my own experience is a case in point on this very theme.

Twenty years down the road now in ministry, I've seen how these Cherith seasons of my own—times when I felt the most unseen and unnoticed—were not only God's way of developing depths of spiritual maturity in me that I didn't yet possess. He was also shielding me from certain people, from certain opportunities, from certain outside influences, as well as from certain traps of the enemy that I had no idea awaited me. Not until much later did the Lord graciously allow me to see that the shadow I'd felt so discouraged inside was actually a holy shield keeping me out of view and under cover.

And you know what hindsight tells me?

It tells me I should have been grateful, not griping, in the middle of it.

> Imagine you're describing this protective quality of Cherith
> to someone younger than you, a sister you're discipling
> one-on-one, over coffee maybe. How could you use your
> own life circumstances to underscore your point?

Let's watch this same scenario play out in another portion of the
Old Testament.

> Turn in your copy of the Scriptures to Exodus 13:17-18, which
> recounts God's dealings with ancient Israel, immediately after
> He miraculously freed them from four hundred years of slavery
> in Egypt. Read these two verses a couple of times, then meet
> me back here to contemplate the following questions:
>
> • How is the proximity of the "land of the Philistines"
>   described?
>
> • What was the Lord's concern in sending His people on this
>   quicker, more convenient route? What was He *shielding*
>   them from?
>
> • What significant landmark would they encounter on the
>   road He'd chosen for them?

What miraculous experience would they have missed had He taken them on the path that was easier and more efficient?

Hang on, because I want you to personalize what you've just read and studied here. But first, consider its ramifications in terms of God's dealings with Israel. The journey from Egypt to Canaan, if the children of Israel had been able to take the direct route, would've taken them roughly eleven days to complete. Just *eleven days*! Instead, God intentionally sent them on an indirect, much more inconvenient, much more time-consuming route. Why?

1. HE WAS PROTECTING THEM.

He was protecting them against the heavily armed forces of the Philistines. God's people were not yet organized well enough to defend themselves successfully against a far superior, far more battle-tested enemy. Furthermore, He was protecting them from themselves. Were they to walk into the teeth of the Philistines, God knew their next step would be a hasty retreat back toward captivity in Egypt. Better the enemy that you know than the one you've never seen and learned how to deal with.

2. HE WAS PUTTING THEM IN POSITION TO SEE HIS POWER.

Geographically, the Red Sea wasn't on the easy route. It was on the less traveled road, the itinerary that took them out of the way. But centuries later—shucks, still today!—we're continuing to talk about the story of God's faithful display of power at the banks of the Red Sea. Had He not hidden them along the highway where most people wouldn't expect them to travel, this particular miracle would never have happened and made it into the history books.

God was *shielding* them from danger. God was *shocking* them with what He could do.

Compare Elijah's experience with that of the children of Israel. What strikes you as similar about God's dealings and purposes with them?

In your own life right now, where do you feel as though God has chosen for you a longer, more inconvenient route for you to travel—in your business, your ministry, your family, your personal development, or some other area that comes to mind? Describe how you've experienced it below.

What has your reaction to it most regularly looked like?

- Impatience?
- Surrender?
- Anger?
- Gratitude?
- Expectation?
- Something else? _____

Maybe, just maybe, many years from now, you'll be digging through a box of old books and stuff, and you'll come across this Bible study. You might even decide, if you remember it fondly enough, that you'd like to do it all over again, and we'll meet together once more in these very same pages. If that happens—and, oh, I hope it does—you'll come across this lesson that we're working through right now. You'll relive again the kinds of difficulties you've written about, the things you've been currently going through where perhaps you're questioning what God is doing.

In hindsight, you'll see that His grace and goodness have been with you all along. Even with everything you've endured and the difficulties you've faced, you'll see the faint outline of His holy shield that was keeping you guarded, protected, and secured. And you'll be able to whisper a heartfelt praise that may feel impossible for you to articulate right now. You'll see that He is good and His plans for you have always and only been good.

Even here.

Under the shadows.

At Cherith.

Zarephath

THE SEASON OF REFINING

FAITH: COMMITTING TO GOD'S PROCESS

#ELIJAHBIBLESTUDY

WEEK THREE
DEALING WITH DEFICIENCY

Here in Zarephath, Elijah is going to be _____. He's going to be
_____. He's going to be _____ for Mount Carmel.

Faith is trusting God enough to go to an _____, unfamiliar place,
and interact with people that it's unusual for us to interact with, so that God
can use us to help inaugurate His move, both in _____ lives and _____ lives.

Elijah could never have known that by yielding to the unfamiliar,
_____ territory where Yahweh sent him that he was
actually helping to tell the entire _____ story.

HOW TO DEAL WITH DEFICIENCY

The widow was _____. She was _____. She was _____.

1. Take _____ inventory.

Sometimes _____ is the hinge upon which a _____ rests.

2. Do not _____.

More than _____ _____ times in Scripture we are told,
"___ ____ fear" or "fear _____."

3. _____.

Maybe you're at the stage where your faith needs to get a _____
—it needs to go to _____.

4. _____ what you _____ you would.

Those sticks you're gathering are not useless. They're the _____ for
the _____ that God fully intends to set in your life.

Video and audio sessions available for purchase
and rent at LifeWay.com/Elijah.

79

UNSETTLED

"Moab has been left quiet since his youth, settled like wine on its dregs. He hasn't been poured from one container to another or gone into exile. So his taste has remained the same, and his aroma hasn't changed."

JEREMIAH 48:11, CSB

Jerry and I celebrated twenty years of marriage by taking a trip to a place we'd never visited before—Napa Valley, California. And you can't really go to Napa, can you, without touring one of its beautiful, operational vineyards?

Every aspect of the vineyard's inner workings was captivating to me. First we walked through the tidy rows of bushy vines and sweet, clustered grapes. From there the guide led us into a large warehouse that held nearly a hundred enormous barrels, each at least ten feet tall and eight feet wide. He explained that after the grapes are plucked by hand and pressed by machine, the thick juice is then poured into these massive containers, capable of collecting up to sixty gallons apiece.

That's where the fermentation process begins. As the grape juice ages, a thick, pungent residue begins to form and separate naturally from it. Then at the right time, they drain the juice through a network of tubes that snake from the bottom of each barrel, leaving nothing behind in the original container except the sour-smelling sediment. The dregs.

This purifying regimen is not performed just once, though. They drain the juice out again. And again. The whole process repeats until all that residue with all its filthy stench is separated and removed. Because if not for this intentional, consistent unsettling from one vessel to the next, the juice can never be rid of those impurities that would keep it from maturing, from developing its clear, soft color and its lusciously sweet smell. Being continually relocated is what refines and prepares it for its intended purpose.

Before reading any further, reread the last paragraph and underline any portions that seem to shimmer with spiritual application. Record the way they resonate with you personally.

Looking back, what have been some of the most dramatic ways that you've experienced this "unsettling" in the past?

What about right now? Describe the main ways you're being unsettled in your current circumstances—shifted from one location to another—physically, emotionally, spiritually, or otherwise.

Now let's go back to that previous paragraph again. This time, circle any words and phrases that describe the *results* of this "intentional, consistent unsettling from one vessel to the next."

Off the top of your head, name some people—either from biblical or modern times—in whom you've seen some of these outcomes take shape because of a shifting that's taken place in their lives.

Comfort and steadiness is what we crave, but overstaying our welcome in one place can rob us of the work God intends to do in us at the next one. In His wise and sovereign way, He often includes seasons of unsettledness where He transfers us out of the comfort and complacency of familiarity and moves us into a new place and position. It's a necessary part of His process.

Each phase represents another refining stage in a divine progression of life. He deposits us into one season, with its own unique set of joys, challenges, people, and problems, and He lets us sit there a while. Pressing us. Sifting us. Purifying us. Then at the right time, when the work that needs to happen there is done, He *unsettles* us—sometimes in a way that feels forcible, sudden, and painful; other times in a nearly undetectable way that is organic, seamless, and can only be pinpointed in hindsight. Either way, He strategically pours us into a new place and space—with new people, with new circumstances, with new life dynamics—knowing this new environment will be the most suitable for whatever He wants to reshape in us next.

Then He does it again, and again—from a heart of love—for as long as we have breath in our lungs. He does it with our best interests in mind. He does it to make us better prepared for the Mount Carmels yet to come. Because if we're never "poured from one container to another," as Jeremiah 48:11 says, we stay unchanged. A foul taste remains in us. A foul aroma sticks to us.

> Go back and read today's lead verse again through the lens of what we've discussed so far today. How much "taste" and "aroma" would be missing from your life if you'd been allowed to stay "settled"—quiet, complacent, and comfortable? Write your thoughts in the margin.
>
> What are some of the "dregs" you'd still be carrying around right now if they hadn't been purified from your life in the unsettling process?

> Jeremiah 48:11 may seem disconnected from our study of Elijah, but there's a sturdy bridge that links it to his narrative. Think back through our two weeks of study. Fill in the blanks with the names of different environments we've already seen Elijah "poured into." The unique dynamics of each location refined him in a unique way.
>
> 1. The mountains of Gilead
> 2. The courts of King _____
> 3. The _____ at Cherith

Open your Bible to 1 Kings 17:7-9. After reading these verses, meet me back here to answer the following questions:

Verse 7. How did Yahweh "unsettle" Elijah at Cherith? What did He allow to happen there?

Verse 8. What did God do in order to solidify to Elijah that he was supposed to move on?

Verse 9. Where's the next place that God poured Elijah into?

By the time we come to verses 7-9, Yahweh was ready to pour Elijah into a new place around new people so that the process of refining could continue. But here's the clear yet difficult task for all of us who want to grow with God, glean the lessons He wants to teach, and move toward fulfilling our unique, divinely mandated purpose. We must *identify* times of divine unsettling so we can release our grasp on one season and willingly move forward to the next, keeping our eyes, ears, and hearts open to receive everything God intends for us there.

For Elijah, and often for us, we can begin to identify a shift by recognizing the following two indicators:

1. THE DRYING BROOK

Elijah wasn't blind. He watched the brook of Cherith slowly dry up before his eyes. As each scorching, rainless day bled into the next, he knew his chances of survival in that secluded spot were going down, until finally the drought had baked his little creek bed into a bone-dry ribbon of dust. Very likely, given his commitment to a lifestyle of fervent prayer—as we saw in James 5—he was consistently discussing his predicament with God—seeking clarity, wisdom, and supply.

"It happened after a while that the brook dried up, because there was no rain in the land."

1 KINGS 17:7

In this reality, we find our first lesson: sometimes we can discern that God is preparing to unsettle us when the resources needed to sustain us in our current position start to shrivel and dry up. Whether it's the money required to support our current venture, the emotional reserves required to invest in a friendship, or the physical energy required to continue the pace of life we've known until now—when these resources start to diminish, look to God. Every day. Ask Him for clarity on why He's allowed this deficiency, then wait for wisdom and direction. Don't let panic set in as you sit beside the drying brook. Instead, "cast your burden upon the LORD and He will sustain you" (Ps. 55:22). As you pray, God will either replenish your supply where you are or, as in Elijah's case, He will keep on letting your brook dry up for the purpose of unsettling you and moving you onward.

Consider this in light of current circumstances in your life. Is there any way you've noticed your resources shrinking (emotional, physical, relational, financial, etc.)?

How have you responded:

- Peace and trust?
- Panic and fear?
- Frustration and irritation?
- A mixture of all three?
- Something else entirely? _____

How might God be using today's lesson to change your perspective and reaction about this? List any observations that indicate He might be intentionally unsettling you in order to shape you, grow you, and prepare you to move forward.

Or try this. Sometimes when I imagine how I'd advise a close friend going through a similar circumstance, I get some much needed clarity for my own life too. How does Elijah's example shape the way you'd counsel a friend today whose "brook" is "drying up"?

If we aren't spiritually discerning, we'll be filled with alarm when our current resources begin drying up. We'll panic instead of trust, become filled with hopelessness instead of eager anticipation about what's to come. But Elijah's narrative helps us see the possibility that when finances fade, when opportunities dwindle, when skills and creativity decline, or when any number of necessities become increasingly unavailable, a new location could likely be awaiting our arrival.

So seek God like Elijah did. Tune your spiritual ears to hear what He might be cuing you toward. And then—listen to me closely now, because here's the part that goes against all our natural reflexes:

Let the brook go dry.

Don't scratch and claw to hang onto the droplets that remain. Rest. Trust. And know that He promises to keep you and care for you and is planning to sustain you in another, more miraculous way. Don't be discouraged. He is unsettling you in order to prepare you, to push you, to move you to the next stage of your journey toward purpose.

2. THE CALL OF GOD

Look up the following verses before contemplating each question.

VERSES	
1 Kings 17:2 1 Kings 17:9 1 Kings 18:1	These verses possess a clear similarity. Can you tell what it is?
1 Kings 17:5 1 Kings 17:10 1 Kings 18:2	These verses reveal Elijah's response to each one, each time. How would you describe it?

We're not told how long Elijah sat beside a dry brook before Yahweh spoke, but we do know at the appropriate time, the same God who'd spoken so clearly to His servant about going to Cherith in the first place now confirmed the next move. Even though Elijah's supply of water

> "Although the Lord has given you bread of privation and water of oppression, He, your Teacher will no longer hide Himself, but your eyes will behold your Teacher. Your ears will hear a word behind you, 'This is the way, walk in it,' whenever you turn to the right or to the left."
>
> ISAIAH 30:20-21

diminished, the promise of Yahweh's nearness and clear direction did not. The same clarity that Elijah had received at other times, he could be confident to receive now. The rain had stopped, but God's word hadn't. At the right time, "the word of the LORD came to him" (1 Kings 17:8).

Looking and listening are critical when you are being unsettled by God's design. Before you can determine if and when to move and where to go, wait for your loving Father's clarity. If He hasn't given it to you, then you don't need to leave Cherith yet. *Wait*. Seek Him in prayer, listening for the gravity of the Spirit's conviction in your soul as He illumines His Word. Seek the counsel of wise mentors and spiritual leaders. Because at the right time, He'll begin to shine a spotlight on the path He's planned for you to take toward Zarephath.

On the graduated scale below, how would you rate your intentionality in patiently waiting and actively looking for God's direction in regard to your current unsettledness?

1	2	3	4	5	6	7	8	9	10

Passive, inactive, impatient, with complaining   Eagerly, patiently, zealously, with thanksgiving

As we prepare to close our devotions today, stop right now and talk to the Lord. Confess any anxiety or panic you may feel in your situation. Ask Him to cause His peace to swell in your heart so you can patiently wait on His direction with confidence and patience.

As the brook dried, Elijah realized what you and I need to realize. His heightened need was not so much of a *problem* as an *opportunity* to hear afresh from God and launch out into a new direction. The prophet didn't manufacture his own plans for relief or wallow in his fears about the future. Instead, he trusted that God would speak just as He'd always spoken, giving him clarity on the next step. He believed the One who'd first called him out of Gilead, and then had given him clear direction to go to Cherith, would continue to be faithful. Elijah wasn't going anywhere until God made clear his next destination. And as soon as he got his orders, he knew what he would do. *Follow them.*

Straight to Zarephath.

ANYWHERE BUT HERE

*"Arise, go to Zarephath, which
belongs to Sidon, and stay there."*

1 KINGS 17:9a

The last couple of years for my extended family have been filled with one difficult circumstance after another. We have really walked through the fire. In fairly quick succession, a number of our close, beloved family members were taken from us by death—eight of them actually, each one hard in its own tragic way. My own sweet mother became diagnosed with a rare form of cancer, for which the doctors could offer few possible remedies. Within a matter of months, she was taken from our presence. Eight months later, my adored mother-in-law unexpectedly and suddenly passed away. They're safe at home now with Jesus, but I miss them so much.

One week after my mother's funeral, in a visit to my own doctors, medical tests confirmed what they suspected and had been telling me. A nodule in my lung, which we'd been keeping our eye on for a while, had grown to an alarming size and would need to be taken out immediately. The invasive surgical procedure to remove the entire upper lobe of my left lung revealed what we were afraid to discover: the nodule was cancerous. Gratefully, the surgery was curative—they were able to get it all—but the recovery and rehabilitation were grueling.

I don't know the details of your personal story, but I do know what all of us went through in the days following my surgery: COVID-19, the global pandemic; followed by the death of an African-American man in police custody, sparking unmitigated racial tensions that flared up into large-scale protests, isolated incidents of rioting, and volatile unrest across America. I'm just saying: whatever amount of life you've experienced, you've been through seasons marked by the fires of hardship and trial. I'm sure of it. Times when you've wanted to be anyplace else.

Anywhere but here.

Elijah felt somewhat the same way—about Zarephath.

The name *Zarephath* comes from a word that means "smelting furnace" or "refining."[1]

Notice the definition of *Zarephath* in the margin. How does this single piece of information parallel with what we've already learned about the way God works maturity and development in His children?

Zarephath was the "furnace" into which Elijah was being sent. Select the kind of effect this element usually has on us. (A few verses that might help you include Ex. 24:17; Isa. 48:10; Zech. 13:9; 1 Cor. 3:13.)

○ Consuming
○ Cleansing
○ Clarifying
○ All of the above

"He knows the way I take; when He has tried me, I shall come forth as gold."

JOB 23:10

Let's keep trekking with Elijah on his journey. Turn to the map in the back of your book and put an X over Zarephath. Draw a connecting link between this new destination and Mount Carmel, then meet me back here.

Elijah would've felt the same way about his "anywhere but here" location that we often feel about ours: *uncomfortable*. The sanctifying work of fire always is. But that's what Zarephath was for Elijah—an introduction to a further season of refining. This location was an unlikely, unusual, and perhaps even distasteful destination for Yahweh to send Elijah.

Several reasons. The first, more general reason is that it was a small village located outside of Israel (did you notice that on the map?) in a population center known for being steeped in pagan idolatry. In other words, the town of Zarephath was a Gentile city, a city governed by Ethbaal, the king of the Sidonians. No doubt you can detect, simply in the sound of the king's name, an audible connection to one of the most well-known of all pseudo-gods in ancient Near Eastern culture. The primary citizens of Zarephath were *Baal worshipers* through and through, whose reverence for their fake deity inflamed them into flagrant, unrestrained acts of religious (should I say, irreligious) fervor.

But that's not the only dark stain that would've made Elijah—or any devoted worshiper of Yahweh—recoil at the directive to go to this town. The second, more specific reason is this: Ethbaal had a daughter named *Jezebel*. And this region of Sidon was her home. Here she'd been reared into the woman who nearly singlehandedly introduced the unhindered worship of Baal among God's people. Once she became the wife of Israel's King Ahab, she used her evil, bullheaded influence to foist Baal worship on the entire nation. She personally supported more than four hundred pagan priests from her own private means and would later hunt down Elijah with designs to kill him for daring to champion the cause of monotheistic worship to the one true God, the worship of Yahweh.

And, yes, that's where God was sending him—to the place where Elijah's chief enemy had been raised.

But wait, I'm getting ahead of myself. Let's stop here and look around Zarephath for a minute, the way it existed at this moment in Elijah's personal life, before Mount Carmel ever came into the picture. Try to think of it as if you were seeing it for the first time through the prophet's own horrified eyes.

Think how this location would have bristled against the things that a Jewish man like Elijah, who absolutely abhorred idolatry, would find familiar and comfortable. What kinds of emotional or mental hurdles would Elijah need to push past in order to obey God by going to Zarephath, both in action and in attitude?

In what ways do you think Elijah could be refined and purified by the smelting furnace of Zarephath's unique dynamics?

For this next question, you'll need to revisit 1 Kings 17:9. How did God tell Elijah to treat his time in Zarephath?

O Visit there
O Stay there
O Pass through it
O Prophesy against it

Think of a place or position where God has set you right now that, for whatever reason, bristles against your comfort. How does this uncomfortable dynamic reshape your perspectives, refine your behaviors, and reframe your attitudes? Be as specific as you can. Prepare to maybe share these thoughts with your study group.

Answering honestly, being neither too hard nor too easy on yourself, how would you describe your response to this unwanted place you're staying in? (Mark any that apply.)

O Constantly on edge, longing for it to change
O Still hopeful, despite the difficulty of it
O Discouraged and, frankly, discontent
O Surrendered to this season of life
O Watching for God's hand in it

The Scriptures contain many examples where God sent an individual to dwell in a place that would have felt uncomfortable and even painful. Often, as was true for Elijah, it wasn't for a short visit but for an extended period of time. For example:

- A place called Bethlehem, and a woman named Ruth (Ruth 1:11-17)
- A place called Egypt, and a man named Joseph (Gen. 37:23-28)
- A place called Jerusalem, and a man named Paul (Acts 20:17-24)
- A place call Patmos, and a man named John (Rev. 1:9-18)

Or a place called Nineveh, and a man named Jonah. You remember Jonah. He lived about a hundred years after Elijah's ministry, during which time Nineveh had developed into one of the principle provinces in the Assyrian Empire. Eventually the Assyrians would wipe the Northern Kingdom of Israel completely off the map.

The leaders of this cruel regime had a reputation for physical and psychological terror, which they freely inflicted on their enemies. Scholars believe it was quite plausible, in fact, that Jonah's hometown had once been in the path of an Assyrian siege. So it's possible he'd seen members of his own family or some of his best friends tortured and killed by ruthless, evil hordes from Nineveh.

The mention of the name "Nineveh" remained a source of raw bitterness, dread, and fear for any card-carrying Israelite like Jonah. And yet Nineveh was where God had clearly called him to go. *Nineveh*. The last thing he ever expected, and certainly the last thing he ever wanted.

> "The word of the LORD came to Jonah the son of Amittai saying, "Arise, go to Nineveh the great city and cry against it, for their wickedness has come up before Me."
>
> **JONAH 1:1-2**

Maybe you remember Jonah's initial response to God's appeal for going to Nineveh. If not, turn to Jonah 1:3 and read it for yourself. Where did Jonah go? Away from what?

Where did Jonah famously end up traveling instead? (See Jonah 1:17.)

Compare Jonah's response to Elijah's. Honestly, which one is most similar to your usual response in regard to God's directives toward a distasteful destination? Jonah's or Elijah's? In what ways?

As I've said before, we can either *resist* or *surrender* to divine disruptions, both in attitude and in action. The Lord leaves us those options. We can either refuse to listen, doubt His sovereignty, fester with bitterness, and miss learning the lessons He wants to teach us in this new location— *OR*—we can "stay there," lean in, and directly engage this place where He's taken us, despite our discomfort, submitting ourselves to the fire in which we will be refined.

> We can either *resist* or *surrender* to divine disruptions, both in attitude and in action.
>
> #ElijahBibleStudy

So right here, right now, I want to revisit the question that you and I dealt with on our first day together in this study, when we agreed with each other about how badly we all want the faith and fire of Elijah in our lives. Remember what we asked ourselves?

ARE WE WILLING TO DO WHAT ELIJAH DID TO GET WHAT ELIJAH GOT?

Knowing now that Zarephath may put you in the line of "fire," what's your sincere answer to this question today? (Answer honestly. This is a no-judgment zone. God hears. He sees. And His grace is sufficient for us.)

Zarephath felt too hot to touch. Elijah couldn't possibly have wanted it any more than he'd wanted Cherith. But think what the Lord was preparing to forge in him from within this furnace: godly maturity, relational wisdom, depth of character, compassion for others, courage in the face of adversity, spiritual openness and preparedness. And since nothing of value in God's kingdom is ever achieved quickly or without cost, this stop on Elijah's journey was going to be worth it. For him and for us.

When you find yourself in a season of trial, in a station or stage of life where you're constantly praying those "anywhere but here" prayers—when you're about to make one of those "anywhere but here" statements—when you can't seem to help yourself from thinking another of those "anywhere but here" thoughts—allow them to simmer in faith instead. Believe that God in His sovereignty has brought you here or is directing you here "so that the proof of your faith, being more precious than gold which is perishable, even though tested by fire, may be found to result in praise and glory and honor at the revelation of Jesus Christ" (1 Pet. 1:7). This place matters. This fire is for refining.

Elijah was headed to Zarephath. There in that city, he would be purified by the circumstances he would face, by the people he would meet, and by the opportunities for divine encounters that he would discover.

And so will we.

ANYONE BUT HER

"Behold, I have commanded a widow
there to provide for you."

1 KINGS 17:9b

Picture this: a hungry, exhausted, unkempt Jewish man sitting by the city gates of a pagan town. Signs of the ongoing drought that have been ravaging the entire region are visible in his face, in his ribs, in the gaunt, dusty condition of his appearance. A quick look around reveals that these same signs are not just his; they're everywhere—in the faces of everyone who passes by, in everyone who lives there. No corner of this territory has been untouched by the drought that's wreaked its havoc beyond the borders of Israel and into the local economy and food supply of Gentile country.

Outside of being an Israelite, Elijah sort of blends in. Yet there's an intensity to his gaze as he watches people milling about, conducting their daily business, chatting about how they're trying to manage underneath this oppressively hot, dry weather that seems to have no letup.

What no one can tell, however, even if they notice him looking around, is that he's looking for someone he's never seen before. The only clue he's been given is that she's a widow, living here in Zarephath, and that she's somehow connected to his future in this town, for as long as God decides to keep him here. Other than that, he's operating on pure, prophetic instinct. He's simply trusting the Lord to point her out to him.

There, is that her? No? What about this one? No.

He sits. He scans. He knows she's out there somewhere.

Then finally, he sees her. He's sure of it. He supernaturally realizes that this lonely, emaciated woman gathering up broken sticks for kindling, her forehead etched with worry and concern, is the one he's been dispatched to find. This woman with the fatigued, desperate look on her face is the same person God has said will provide sustenance for Elijah in the midst of this drought.

THIS woman, Lord? This hungry, helpless, Gentile woman?

Oh, dear God, anywhere but *here*. And anyone but *her*.

Read the following paragraph carefully, underlining the socioeconomic characteristics of widows who lived during this time period.

A widow had no identity, sense of belonging, or security. During this famine, she and her son would have been starving. The city gate was where people could possibly help her—the place where life change was possible for someone without a means to provide more for herself than the last bit of flour and oil she had left.

The weakest, most vulnerable people on the socioeconomic ladder during Elijah's day were women. But the marginalization that every woman experienced, solely because of her gender, was heightened even further if the woman happened to be unmarried; even worse if she were widowed. A widow truly existed on the fringes of society, living without any of the protections and benefits of kinship. Having no male companion as her representative, her access to the public square was functionally zero.

So not only had God commanded Elijah to go to a *place* that seemed unreasonable, He'd also called him to make connections there with a *person* who was thought to be nothing. Insignificant. Of little to no value.

And to cap off the complete absurdity of this unsavory situation, God hadn't sent Elijah to Zarephath to be the strong man who would provide for *her*. The widow had been tapped by Yahweh to be the avenue of provision for *him*.

Elijah was a rugged Jewish man of the mountains. How might his interaction with the widow specifically refine him in the following areas?

- Pride
- Prejudice
- Doubt
- Compassion
- What else comes to mind? _____

A lot of people find it hard to receive even so much as a compliment, much less receive tangible help from others, especially others they feel should be receiving from *them*. On a scale of 1-10—with 1 being easy; 10 being hard— circle the number that corresponds to your difficulty with *receiving* from someone else's generosity.

1	2	3	4	5	6	7	8	9	10

Easy   Hard

Which reason (or reasons) would you specify as being the primary cause for why receiving assistance from others or causing them inconvenience is hard for you to accept?

○ I like others to view me as helping them, not the other way around.
○ My pride hinders me from being authentic and open about my need.
○ Other people's problems always seem more pressing than mine.
○ I think I secretly tend to bask in feeling superior to others.
○ It's easier to hide my lack and pretend to be OK.
○ I just don't want to be a burden on anyone.
○ Something else: _____

Could this be one of the places where you need the fire of refining? How so? Which pieces of this attitude need to be burned up and consumed?

In Cherith, Elijah was on the receiving end of God's miraculous provision for maybe a year and a half. He was accustomed now to being in need, to feeling dependent, to knowing what it was like not having sufficient resources to care for himself.

See "Digging Deeper II" article on page 112.

And yet this new assignment in the furnace of Zarephath would've refined him in another unique way. Because it's one thing for a flock of birds to bring you meat and bread. No one else is there to witness the transaction, to see you up-close at your worst and neediest. It's sort of like receiving a financial gift from someone you don't know and may never see again or getting a glowing comment of encouragement from a post on your social media. Anonymity doesn't require authenticity. You don't have to be real with ravens.

Anonymity doesn't require authenticity.

#ElijahBibleStudy

But you do have to be real with a widow when she's standing right there in front of you, when she's the one who's providing you room and board and can see your need at close range. At Zarephath, you graduate to a harder test. Zarephath requires vulnerability. Zarephath involves a baring of soul that can't be masked or covered with makeup. Zarephath leaves no space for being less than honest about what's harbored in your heart.

Zarephath cuts you down to size.

Not only would Elijah's pride, self-reliance, and any sense of supremacy be purified during his relationship with this person—this "anyone but her" person—but by submitting to Zarephath, Elijah was being positioned for things more impactful and far-reaching than he could ever have imagined.

1. A PARTICIPANT IN GOD'S BIGGER PLAN

This encounter the Lord set in motion between Elijah and a Gentile widow pointed to much more than simply a famine survival strategy for one solitary man.

Turn to Luke 4:24-26, where Jesus spoke to the people of Nazareth many centuries after Elijah lived. Record the surprising insight that the Messiah shares.

Now read the apostle Paul's writing in the margin and consider it in light of Jesus' statement. Then meet me back here to answer this question: How did Elijah's interaction with a Gentile widow begin to reveal God's overarching story of redemption?

Elijah would have been startlingly aware of all the many destitute widows who were foraging for food on Israel's streets. He likely wondered why God would send him to a *Gentile* widow, when there were so many Jewish ones in need. And yet God sovereignly chose a widow outside of the boundaries of Israel to make a broader point, to provide a foundation for His message of universal redemption.

In Zarephath, God would testify that His ultimate plan for the redemption of humanity didn't extend to only one group of people but to everyone— the disenfranchised, marginalized, and forgotten. This encounter would begin to reveal His heart toward all people of all ages, in every demographic. Elijah's connection to the widow would model the fact that no one has a monopoly on God's grace, that His redemptive plan is much larger than one single nationality or class. It includes people from every tongue, tribe, nation, and station.

We know this concept now as the gospel, a spiritual reality that is far wider in vantage point than anything Elijah could have fathomed. He couldn't have known in the moment that this thread of his story was being woven into a beautiful tapestry with prophetic significance in God's broader plan and purposes. In Zarephath, Yahweh wasn't doing a work in Elijah's life only; He was demonstrating the purpose that He came into the world to accomplish.

Turn to Acts 10:34-35. Reading these two verses, you'll hear the apostle Peter coming to terms with this same, inclusive message of the gospel. Think of it now in terms of the modern world where we live. In what ways do you see this message still needing to be fully absorbed?

"For you are all sons of God through faith in Christ Jesus. For all of you who were baptized into Christ have clothed yourselves with Christ. There is neither Jew nor Greek, there is neither slave nor free man, there is neither male nor female; for you are all one in Christ Jesus."

GALATIANS 3:26-28

No one has a monopoly on God's grace . . . His redemptive plan is much larger than one single nationality or class. It includes people from every tongue, tribe, nation, and station.

#ElijahBibleStudy

For another biblical account that emphasizes this principle, spend time reading and meditating on Philip's encounter with an Ethiopian eunuch (Acts 8:25-40).

Make it personal. Where do you perhaps fall short, allowing prejudices that you've been taught or have picked up along the way to prevent you from being as open toward others as you ought to be?

When Elijah humbly surrendered to the furnace of Zarephath, not only was he positioned for his own refinement, but he was becoming a key player in the Lord's eternal purposes. Without even needing to understand what God was up to, Elijah's willingness to follow His lead—establishing relationship with an "anyone but her" person—linked him into an experience that glorified God and is still speaking to us today.

How does this reminder about God's larger plan add perspective, even value, to the people the Lord has strategically placed in your path right now? How does it help you rest in God's sovereignty?

2. A PARTNER IN GOD'S MIRACULOUS PROVISION

Yes, it started with Elijah being meek and humble. It started with being needy and vulnerable. It started with choosing to present himself empty—as empty as the widow woman he flagged down in the streets of Zarephath. The emaciation in her eyes would detect the same emaciation in his. The hollowness in her stomach would growl in chorus with his own. Elijah's authenticity would be how God taught him that he wasn't so different from this Gentile widow after all. They both needed water; they both needed bread.

But emptiness, when acknowledged, is often what builds bridges to others. It intersects you with someone else's lack, where God can then use you as a catalyst for their own encounter with Him. By the time we

ELIJAH

reach tomorrow's lesson, bread and oil will miraculously start to multiply in the widow's house. Elijah's faith is going to turn into an exciting ministry opportunity. From a place of needing to be fed himself, he will introduce others to the God who can feed them too. This is what Zarephath teaches us. Being honest about our own lack comes first, then we get the privilege of becoming a partner in God's miraculous provision.

Sister, maybe you thought the scarce, lacking, dried-up places in your life would turn out to be the reasons why God *couldn't* use you, why He *couldn't* do anything significant through you. But these points of marked emptiness are actually the keys that open doors of ministry for you and of God's miracles through you. It's where your deficiencies line up for you to intersect with destiny.

With *anyone but her.*

For Elijah, his own need is what built a bridge to the widow's need. And Yahweh used it as the basis of a miracle for both of them.

> As you close today's lesson, use the following short prayer as a catalyst to form your own conversation with the Lord.
>
> *Lord, I repent today of any pride—of any unspoken sense of superiority—of any callousness that has kept me from connecting with certain people. Refine me, Father. Sanctify me until I reflect the image of Your Son, Jesus. By Your Spirit, give me perspective and vision to see the bigger story that You're trying to tell through my life. And when I can't see it, help me to trust. Thank You that my emptiness is not in vain. Tenderize my heart to live in authenticity, humility, and yielded surrender while I'm here in Zarephath. In Jesus' name, amen.*

WHAT I SEE, WHAT HE SAYS

"We look not at the things which are seen,
but at the things which are not seen; for
the things which are seen are temporal, but
the things which are not seen are eternal."

2 CORINTHIANS 4:18

These next few verses are too breathtaking and unforgettable not to be read in their entirety. I've printed them here for you. Linger in this passage and soak in every detail of God's power. Watch Him use Elijah, after seeing the widow gathering wood nearby, to provide hope and peace where there had been neither, to provide food and water where both had been in diminished supply. Most of all, watch Him care enough to introduce Himself to one woman—forgotten by others but known and seen by a loving Father.

> ¹⁰ Elijah called to her and said, "Please bring me a little water in a cup and let me drink." ¹¹ As she went to get it, he called to her and said, "Please bring me a piece of bread in your hand." ¹² But she said, "As the LORD your God lives, I don't have anything baked—only a handful of flour in the jar and a bit of oil in the jug. Just now, I am gathering a couple of sticks in order to go prepare it for myself and my son so we can eat it and die." ¹³ Then Elijah said to her, "Don't be afraid; go and do as you have said. But first make me a small loaf from it and bring it out to me. Afterward, you may make some for yourself and your son, ¹⁴ for this is what the LORD God of Israel says, 'The flour jar will not become empty and the oil jug will not run dry until the day the LORD sends rain on the surface of the land.'" ¹⁵ So she proceeded to do according to the word of Elijah. Then the woman, Elijah, and her household ate for many days. ¹⁶ The flour jar did not become empty, and the oil jug did not run dry, according to the word of the LORD he had spoken through Elijah.

1 KINGS 17:10b-16, CSB

See, wasn't that good? On the lines below, write out any phrases or details from this passage that speak prominently to you. (Feel free to use the empty space in the margin if you need more room.)

Now think through and respond to the following questions:

• What do the opening few words of verse 11 tell you about the widow's heart?

• How did she describe the status of her food supply in verse 12?

• What had she concluded about her and her son's future?

• What similar realities had Elijah faced at Cherith?

OK, for just a moment now, travel with me to Houston, Texas, circa 1980, where a pastor's wife named Dodie was diagnosed with liver cancer. She was only forty-six years old. (I can say "only" now because forty-six feels pretty personal to me these days. Don't ask me why.) Ms. Dodie still had teenagers at home. She and her husband were busy leading a vibrant local church. She didn't have time for cancer. People needed her. She had lots to do. But on the day she was diagnosed, doctors gave her two weeks to live.

You heard me right. Two *WEEKS*.

But today, some forty *YEARS* later, she is not only alive but is cancer-free. Her healing has been so complete, in fact, that many people have doubted if she was really that sick in the first place. But she's got the exploratory images and paperwork to prove it. Everyone close to her and to that situation would tell you Dodie is a walking, breathing miracle.

But that doesn't mean the journey to healing wasn't long, dark, and difficult. In her loneliest days, when hope seemed totally barren, she felt she was left with no choice but to turn wholeheartedly to God—more than ever!—trusting Him with her children, with her ministry, with her unfinished work, with her life.

This was her *Cherith*.

Her health whittled away like the water in Elijah's brook.

But remember what Cherith is for—*separating, sustaining, surprising, shielding*. This experience with cancer forced her into an intimacy with God that only a Cherith survivor can fully understand. Out of this place, like springs of water in the desert, came an explosion of ministry that has impacted millions of people around the world—including my own mother. Each day during my mom's cancer odyssey, she listened to an audio recording of Dodie quoting the Scriptures that had been the soundtrack of her own journey decades ago. These unchanging truths from God's Word had become cemented into Ms. Dodie's soul during her darkest days, which she intentionally recorded and handed down to future generations of sufferers who could be blessed by her soothing and powerful delivery of what she'd learned. And of what God has said.

Is there someone in your sphere of influence right now whose circumstances mirror something you've faced before and survived? Write his or her name here, and summarize the situation as that person has described it to you.

Think back. Which of God's specific promises carried you through that season?

Have you taken the opportunity to proactively share these truths with the person whose name you recorded? If not, consider the reasons why. What's keeping you from making this divine point of contact with them?

○ I'm too shy/afraid/awkward.
○ I don't want to embarrass them.
○ I'm too busy to make the time.
○ I'm preoccupied with other stuff.
○ I don't want a long conversation.
○ I never thought about it.
○ I didn't keep a record of what God taught me at my Cherith.
○ All of the above

Look back again at 1 Kings 17:14, where Elijah gave the widow hope amid her desperate condition. Write down the first clause from verse 14 below.

What do these words tell you about Elijah's perspective regarding the widow's circumstances?

In the despair of the moment, this widow was consumed by what she could see. Elijah, however, reported what God had *said*.

WHAT WE *SEE* / WHAT HE *SAYS*

Now put down your pen and just read the next few paragraphs with a prayerful perspective. This "what we *see* / what He *says*" disparity reveals one of the major distinctions that should be readily apparent between people who do not know God and those who do. What God says pinpoints the hinge that separates hope from hopelessness, possibility from impossibility. His statement "Thus says the LORD God of Israel" and the perspective it represents changed the entire trajectory of the widow's story.

What God says pinpoints the hinge that separates hope from hopelessness, possibility from impossibility.

#ElijahBibleStudy

Elijah's time in Cherith is what enabled his faith reflex to be so easily ignited during his interaction with the widow. He seemed almost to jump at the chance to introduce God's provision and promise to her. He didn't minimize her lack or pretend it wasn't real, but he also didn't rehearse it or stew on it. Instead he emphasized the *word of the Lord* that applied to her specific circumstance.

The same is true for you, my friend.

> "He comforts us in all our affliction, so that we may be able to comfort those who are in any kind of affliction, through the comfort we ourselves receive from God."
>
> **2 CORINTHIANS 1:4, CSB**

Among the reasons for why God has placed you in your office or in that classroom, in your neighborhood or on the board of that organization, after having gone through the Cherith experiences that He's allowed into your life, is because they create a point of contact between the promises of God that you've hidden in your heart and the people around you who are hurting. They need to know the truth of God and how to accurately appropriate it. Their perspective needs to be renewed by the encouraging, reinvigorating promises of God.

Will you succumb to their fear or will you help elevate them to God's truth?

Impossibility is God's starting point. The people who live and work around you, even the ones who only infrequently pass in and out of your life—each of them needs to know that "with God all things are possible" (Matt. 19:26). Part of your privilege as His child is to keep this limitless perspective and expectation continually before your eyes so that His Word is continually in your mouth, poised to deliver His encouragement to others.

Listen to me: Zarephath strategically brings you face to face with someone else's impossibility—the terminal diagnosis, the unreachable child, the failing marriage, the crippling depression. Hear them and sincerely empathize when they tell you what they *see*, but don't leave the conversation without inserting what their omniscient, omnipresent, sovereign, promise-keeping God *says*.

If you don't, who will?

So, friend, here are the questions that today's whole lesson hinges upon: (1) Are you investing time into searching God's Word—discovering His heart, His perspective, and His promises that apply to us today—so that you know what He has said about situations like these? Or (2) are you caught up and swept away in the same vortex of hopelessness that the people in front of you are feeling, where you can only commiserate with them in their pain but are ill-equipped to speak the truth in love, appropriately inserting God's vantage point into the conversation at every opportunity?

Take these questions and your heart responses to the Lord in prayer. Use the margin as journaling space for your honest thoughts. Ask Him to show you how He has called you to be an "Elijah"—a spokesperson for His promises—to every "widow" you come into contact with. Ask Him to make your commitment to His Word so strong that it not only governs your behavior, speech, and attitude, but also spills from your lips instinctively. Regularly. Naturally.

Zarephath's widows need a word from the Lord. And you, modern-day Elijah, need to know it so you can share it. This is Zarephath's challenge to you. To me. To us.

Hope hinges on it.

As you wrap up today, here are just a few of the sweet, strong promises of God that you can use immediately to encourage others in their struggles and distresses. When you have time, look up several or all of these verses, being careful to consider the context around them. See if God may already be lining up one or more of them to speak *precisely* to a need that you're familiar with in someone else's life:

- Deuteronomy 31:6
- Joshua 1:9
- Psalm 23:4
- Proverbs 29:25
- Isaiah 41:10
- Lamentations 3:57

- Daniel 10:12
- Luke 12:7
- John 14:27
- Hebrews 13:6
- 1 Peter 3:14
- Revelation 2:10

Who can you call or email to share one of these assurances with, helping to calm their anxious hearts and stay anchored in truth?

OPEN IN PRAYER

"The woman said to Elijah, 'Now I know
that you are a man of God and that the
word of the LORD in your mouth is truth.'"

1 KINGS 17:24

I want us to start today's study by diving into some devotional questions
for you to think about. Here we go.

If you were teaching an elementary-age Sunday School
class, how would you define prayer to your students?
(Remember, these are kids you're talking to.)

What's your own personal relationship with prayer? (Circle
any that apply.)

- I feel confident when I pray.
- Prayer tends to disappoint me.
- I do it because I know I should.
- I find prayer to be uncomfortable.
- Prayer is a priority to me.
- Something else _____

Circle the option that best describes the current status of
your prayer life.

- Formal
- Infrequent
- Consistent but not daily
- Knee-jerk reaction to crisis
- Fervent, passionate, and ongoing
- Habitual, like a mealtime blessing

On the scales below—with 1 being really stiff; 10 being really natural—circle the numbers that correspond to your comfort level with:

1	2	3	4	5	6	7	8	9	10

Private prayer (alone with God)

1	2	3	4	5	6	7	8	9	10

Public prayer (in front of others)

Do you typically struggle with making larger, supernatural, miraculous requests of God? Why?

Do you feel uncomfortable asking Him for things that seem small or insignificant? Why?

Today's last lesson from Zarephath is about this all-important issue of prayer. That's because "after these things"—after God had been daily, miraculously providing meal service for Elijah and the widow—the Bible says something terrible happened (1 Kings 17:17). Her son came down with a severe illness serious enough that he died from it. And in the wake of this tragedy, we're about to see an additional aspect of Elijah's spiritual life and character being refined and fortified for future use.

Think how unconscionable this stunning turn of events must have seemed to them. To both of them. They thought they'd dodged the famine bullet. God had been remarkably feeding them, enough for them to live on every single day, presumably *to keep them alive!* But now it all seemed for nothing. This mother's greatest fear had become her reality anyway.

And she immediately started assigning blame.

Turn to 1 Kings 17:18-20. Focusing for now on just verse 18, where the widow was hysterical with grief, paraphrase her outburst against Elijah.

When was the last time you were unjustly accused of something, and what was your response to it?

○ Defended myself
○ Kept quiet
○ Passed blame off to another person
○ Something else _____

> "He cried out to the LORD and said, 'LORD my God, have you also brought tragedy on the widow I am staying with by killing her son?'"
>
> 1 KINGS 17:20, CSB

I am intrigued and challenged by Elijah's reaction to the widow's accusations. Instead of defending himself, instead of returning her emotional volley, instead of taking offense at her attack on his "man of God" reputation, he was mainly silent, calm, and compassionate. He didn't react in any of the ways I usually do when shade is thrown my direction. As proof that he'd absorbed well the lessons of Gilead, Cherith, and now Zarephath, he looked away from his accuser and upward to the Lord.

Elijah immediately took his concerns into prayer.

This tells me that one of the outworkings of God's process of maturity in our lives should be a more natural reflex into fervent prayer at our most awkward and unfair moments. Instead of being rattled by people's reactions and by the ugly, cutting things they may say, our own instinctive reactions can flow from what the Father has been continually maturing in us and teaching us about the beautiful, powerful exchange of prayer. We immediately:

- Exchange pride for humility;
- Exchange self-assurance for reliance;
- Exchange independence for divine dependence;
- Exchange doubt for firmness of faith;
- Exchange panic for peace.

Progressively at each stage of his journey thus far, Elijah has made this exchange: first in Gilead, then in Ahab's court, then at Cherith, and increasingly during his time in Zarephath. And that's what we can expect too. The fruit of all these lessons will become ripe in moments of crisis.

> In this list of "exchanges," circle the one that speaks to where you see God working the most in your life right now.
>
> What practical, deliberate action can you take in the next twenty-four hours that shows you're working toward this exchange—right there in the most pressing circumstance or relationship struggle you're facing?

As God matures and refines us, life's crises won't be as capable of flipping the switch inside us that rams us into fear and anxiety mode. Instead, they will trigger an innate reaction within us to call out, to cry out, to the Lord. To trust Him. To rely on His sovereignty. To reach out in faith, believing our God is "able to do exceedingly abundantly above all that we ask or think" (Eph. 3:20, NKJV).

Elijah made this exchange. We see it here in Zarephath. We see its heat already building in his life, showing signs that it can stand up to the intense scrutiny yet to come. The lessons he learned about prayer *in this fire* at Zarephath will teach him how to *call down fire* on Mount Carmel. Let's see if we can walk away with three lessons in prayer that Elijah's example teaches us.

1. TAKE THE WHOLE PROBLEM TO GOD IN PRAYER.

When Elijah scooped up the widow's lifeless son, he was literally carrying the problem to the Lord. He was presenting to Him the entire, devastating reality that he'd just witnessed, in all its stark, dismal truth. There would be no masking the issue, no denial of what was happening, no sugarcoating of details to make the gravity of the scene any more palatable. This was no time for pious rituals or platitudes, but simply for going all-in with the One who alone, and no other, could infuse life-giving power into this situation.

"He said to her, 'Give me your son.'"

1 KINGS 17:19a

Is there a glaring need or battle in your life right now that you haven't fully presented to God in prayer? Use the space below to repent of the pride that has kept you from releasing everything to God and then get real about it. Bring it on. Bring it all.

2. CULTIVATE A PLACE OF PRIORITY IN PRAYER.

"He took him from her arms, carried him to the upper room where he was staying, and laid him on his bed."

1 KINGS 17:19b, NIV

Many scholars believe that this "upper room" where Elijah took the body of the dead child was likely the space in the house where he'd done a lot of praying already. He was accustomed to going there for the purpose of prayer. It was his "War Room," to use some imagery we're familiar with, where he regularly met with God.

I'll be the first to say there's nothing magic about a specific place when it comes to praying. We can pray in the den, pray in the kitchen, pray in our bedroom, pray in the backyard. If we're to "pray without ceasing" like Scripture teaches (1 Thess. 5:17), we're sure to cover a lot of ground throughout the course of our daily prayer life. But having a specific *place* of prayer can signify the *priority* we've placed on prayer. That's the point (see Matt. 6:6). Elijah knew exactly where to take that boy, straight up into the room where God had shown up so powerfully so many times.

"He stretched himself upon the child three times, and called to the LORD and said, 'O LORD my God, I pray You, let this child's life return to him.' The LORD heard the voice of Elijah, and the life of the child returned to him and he revived."

1 KINGS 17:21-22

What do you consider to be the value of a set-aside and go-to place where you can regularly run to God in prayer?

3. EXPECT GOD TO ANSWER UNREASONABLE PRAYERS.

Elijah's audacious prayer request came with no blueprint for him to follow. Apart from the ancient biblical account of Enoch, who wasn't even dead when God just "took him" from Earth to raptured glory (Gen. 5:24), there's not a single record from any earlier Scripture that hints at a precedent for a resurrection prayer. And there's certainly no prescription for his decision to lay himself across the boy's body. In fact, according to Jewish law, touching a human corpse resulted in a seven-day quarantine (see Num. 19:11). Ordinarily, Elijah would've considered this physical contact with a dead body as being exceptionally vile and unclean. And yet his compassion for this family, a compassion forged in the fire of his own need and suffering, trampled all protocols. He blazed his own trail, launching a prayer so bold into the heavenlies that no one else in recorded biblical history had ever employed it before.

Only one thing can account for this level of expectation and trust in the power of Almighty God. The process of being galvanized in Gilead, Cherith, and Zarephath had turned spiritual concept into spiritual concrete. Elijah didn't just *have* faith anymore. Elijah *lived* faith.

His faith had caught fire.

> **If you were to make an unreasonable, unthinkable prayer today, what do you think it would be? (You're not limited to one. Think of as many as you can.)**

> **Then pray it. Do it right now. Let your faith be set ablaze.**

I almost hesitate to interrupt you. Ending this lesson on prayer, by being in prayer, is such a fitting way to transition from the first half of our study to the next. Praying at a new level of believing faith feels like the perfect way of capturing what God has been pouring into our lives throughout these three strong weeks. Thank you for hanging in with me this far.

This is what we want, isn't it? Whatever it takes to get here. We want faith that can believe God for moments like this one, when Elijah walked back into that widow's house, with her son walking right beside him. "Now I know that you are a man of God," she exclaimed, not knowing which one to hug the hardest. "The word of the LORD in your mouth is truth" (1 Kings 17:24).

Our lives can compel those closest to us to *know* our God reigns. Our faith can excite them to discover the power of God for themselves, even as we continue to grow and mature, developing strength and fortitude in the process. We're certainly going to need it.

Mount Carmel is coming.

REFINED BY FAMILY

Theologian and Bible scholar F. B. Meyer writes:

> Many a man might bear himself as a hero and saint in the solitudes of Cherith or on the heights of Carmel, and yet wretchedly fail in the home life of Zarephath. It is one thing to commune with God in the solitudes of nature and perform splendid acts of devotion and zeal for Him in the presence of thousands, but it is quite another to walk with Him day by day in the midst of a home with its many calls for constant forgetfulness of self.[2]

For roughly eighteen months, Elijah had been alone at Cherith learning to live within the context and cadence of solitude. Adjusting to this dynamic of separateness had steadily refined the prophet in one way, but the new dynamics of Zarephath would refine him in another way, one which extended beyond the scope of simple geography. For here in Zarephath, he would shift from living alone to existing within the context of family, making his home with a single mother and her son.

This new dynamic, with its daily mundane demands and relational nuances, would methodically and intentionally wean him from the ingrown tendencies that can come from unrestrained solitude. He would transition from a life in which he could be concerned only about his own needs to a season in which awareness and thoughtfulness of others would be essential.

The constant give and take of family life, even a surrogate family, is precisely the dynamic that God often uses to mold us in a unique way. Solitude may be beautiful and restful, but if allowed to become unbalanced, it can also make us self-absorbed—stuck inside our own thoughts and needs, unconcerned and unable to walk in relationship with others. Too much time alone can cause us to become hardened, narrow, desensitized, and one-dimensional. People become little more than a bother or a threat, a problem we're forced to bend our plans and agendas around, instead of a holy opportunity and gift to relate with.

Have you ever noticed that it often seems easier to sense the peace and presence of God and exhibit the fruit of His Spirit when you're alone? When you're off on a retreat or rocking on the back porch, perhaps overlooking a placid lake while sipping hot coffee and listening to worship music from a self-curated playlist. In solitude, there are no interruptions, with nothing and no one pulling us away or challenging our choices. No compromise is required or expectations unmet. Patience is not required or cultivated. In solitude, we only need to consider our own needs, desires, and struggles.

But when there are dishes to be done, household projects to tackle, problems to solve, relational dilemmas to disentangle, people to serve and prioritize, or last-minute homework help to provide, much more vigilance is required to keep that same awareness of God's presence and to live in light of it.

The fruit of God's Spirit—virtues like patience, gentleness, and kindness—are not cultivated in contexts where they are not required. Part of the reason for why "God sets the lonely in families" (Ps. 68:6, NIV) is to produce in us what solitude cannot.

The most beautiful and astounding opportunity for experiencing this dynamic, for every believer in any season or situation in life, is the family of God into which we are born when we place faith in Jesus. By His grace we are "no longer foreigners and strangers, but fellow citizens with the saints, and members of God's household" (Eph. 2:19, CSB).

We are a part of a family. *His* family. The household of God.

So as we navigate life with one another in the context of *church* life, we are essentially navigating *family* life, where we have the ongoing opportunity for development, maturity, and the achievement of greater purity and selflessness of motive. When we are firmly planted and functioning actively within the family, we are refined; our inner lives are pruned; our character is developed; our demanding sense of self is progressively quieted. Even if we live alone, the body of Christ is the context where we are never alone. Instead our brothers and sisters become a part of the story that God is telling through our lives. These fellow sojourners are our family members, and the Father is developing all of us as we relate to each other. So, sister, let's not forsake "our own assembling together, as is the habit of some" (Heb. 10:25).

You belong here. This is your home. We are your family.

Carmel

EXPOSING THE COUNTERFEIT

WEEK FOUR

DON'T DROP THE BALL

There's a _____ that sits right between Elijah's time in Zarephath and his coming experience on Mount Carmel, and this link, this bridge, is _____.

Stop downplaying the _____ of your position. Stop undervaluing how critical and purposeful your current posture is. You are _____, right where you are.

God's hand is on you wherever He has _____ you, to be used for His purposes and His glory. Keep your spiritual eyes open, and don't _____ _____ _____.

There's something to be said, not only about being in a _____ position, but also about making an unwavering pledge, having a fierce _____ of the things of God.

What are you _____ doing to make sure you are _____ the _____ of God in this generation?

Just in doing your job, that _____ _____ leads to a moment of _____ _____.

Video and audio sessions available for purchase and rent at LifeWay.com/Elijah.

115

RAIN AND FIRE

"Now it happened after many days that
the word of the LORD came to Elijah in the
third year, saying, 'Go, show yourself to Ahab,
and I will send rain on the face of the earth.'"

1 KINGS 18:1

Think back to the last time you had to wait for something, every day, for an extended period of time. An important email into your inbox? A call about the results of a job interview? Word from your grown son or daughter about medical tests on your grandchild? Remember how you felt—going to bed each night, then waking up each morning, hoping *surely* this would be the day you'd hear something. You didn't know if you could wait much longer.

Every day for three and a half years—roughly 1,277 days—the people of Israel squinted into the sun-streaked skies wondering when in the world this drought would break. Scientists who study such things can measure the depleting effects of drought on crops, soil, and water supply after as little as *one week* of no rain, much less a year, two years, three years. What they can't measure, only observe, is the mental and emotional toll it takes—especially in an agrarian society like the Israel of Elijah's day— the daily stress of trying to wring out enough resources to care for your family, fields, and flocks, when your whole economy hinges on it.

It's why King Ahab, as I shared with you in this week's video session, took the extreme action of going out *himself* as part of a surveying team, along with his trusted (and God-fearing) advisor Obadiah, in desperate hopes of finding enough grass to keep the livestock alive.

Into this state of events and emotions—where *every day* they wished for rain—the "word of the LORD came to Elijah," declaring that He was calling an end to this divinely orchestrated attempt at getting His people's attention.

Yahweh was preparing to send down the rain.

In this season of your life, is there something you've been fixated on—something you've desired in the same way the Israelites desired rain? Something relational? Financial? Material? Work-related? Family-related? What is it?

Why do you think you want it as much as you do? How do you think receiving it would positively impact your life?

Now shift your perspective. What has the delay in receiving it given to you or produced in you?

What opportunities has this unmet need/want presented?

What relationships or encounters has it fostered?

What uptick in spiritual intimacy has it facilitated?

As we've learned from Elijah's life, seasons of waiting—seasons of want—can be golden opportunities for growth, development, preparation, and refining. When we surrender them to the Lord, when we receive them as an importantly patient, painful part of a useful sanctifying process, He causes them to produce things of great value in our lives. Faith.

Seasons of waiting—seasons of want—can be golden opportunities for growth, development, preparation, and refining.

#ElijahBibleStudy

> "When the earth experiences Your judgments the inhabitants of the world learn righteousness. Though the wicked is shown favor, He does not learn righteousness; He deals unjustly in the land of uprightness, and does not perceive the majesty of the LORD."
>
> ISAIAH 26:9b-10

Resilience. Godly perspective. Deeper, more personal intimacy with Him. There is *purpose* in the deprivation.

Turn to 1 Kings 18:17-18, which reports on the first face-to-face encounter between Ahab and Elijah in three years. In reading the words they shared, compare and contrast the perspective that each man possessed regarding this ordeal.

• Ahab (v. 17)

• Elijah (v. 18)

Now read the two verses from Isaiah 26 in the margin, and answer the following questions:

• What are God's "judgments" designed to instill in people's hearts?

• Consider the concept of "learn[ed] righteousness." What does this mean, and what does it look like?

• How do you see Ahab's reaction mirrored in the three closing statements of verse 10?

The revelation of Jehovah's majesty to a double-minded nation and its hard-hearted king was the primary objective of the consequences they had suffered. Above all other outcomes, this was the goal He intended to be the outworked climax of the drought.

In other words, it wasn't really about the rain at all. The lack of water was just for context. The drought conditions were the result of Israel's failure to adhere to the covenant, yes, but they were simultaneously a catalyst designed to turn the heart of the nation back to Him and to highlight His deity.

So after three difficult years, the people and their king understandably thought their greatest need was for something to bathe in and cook in and grow their food in. But this was not Yahweh's most pressing desire for them. Their greatest need—always our greatest need—was for God Himself. Elijah knew this. And now the people were about to know it too.

The prophet, having learned from Gilead, and from Cherith, and from Zarephath, and from the word of the Lord growing stronger and clearer and more vibrant in his heart at each step along the way, was ready now to press the issue. The time had come for Ahab and for Israel to climb up to the precipice of the mountain and get a firsthand view of what they didn't even realize was their most pressing, primary need.

Before rain, *fire!*

> Move your finger down now to 1 Kings 18:19, where Elijah declared the terms of his proposal, before there was to be any rain.
>
> Who was to come?
> • All _____
> • Four hundred prophets of _____
> • Four hundred fifty prophets of _____
> • Those who were supported by _____
>
> Where were they to assemble?
> • Mount _____

With this deal struck between Elijah and Ahab, the hungry and dehydrated people of Israel marched in solemn groups toward the towering mountain known as Carmel, jutting more than 1,750-feet above sea level. Picturesque against the Mediterranean coastline, it was well south of Zarephath, where Elijah had been, and a stout northwesterly distance from Israel's capital city of Samaria.

> Turn again to your map in the back and locate where Mount Carmel stands. Draw a line from Samaria to its location.

After such a long time of dryness, everybody believed the end of the drought must finally be at hand. Their eyes were peeled to the heavens looking for rain. With this mass call and holy movement to the mountain, the conversations along the roads and trails leading up to Carmel must have buzzed with excited anticipation. The last time they'd heard from the prophet Elijah, he had called off the rain. Surely he'd returned now to call it back on. To slake their thirst. To raise his hands toward the heavens from the top of Mount Carmel and appeal to Yahweh for the clouds to open up once again. To give them what they *wanted*.

But the people were soon to see that they hadn't been called up here to get a desired taste of *water* from heaven but a needed blast of *fire* from heaven. They knew what they wanted, but God knew what they needed first—a fresh revelation and experience with Him—even above the thing that they perceived to be their greatest need at the moment.

As you pray for the remedies and solutions that your heart most desires, remember that your loving, all-knowing Father will often answer first with fire, giving you a fresh revelation of Him above all else. In the moment His answer may seem disjointed or disconnected, like the heat of flames in a time of drought. But choose to trust Him even as you continue to wait for rain.

"When you pray, say: 'Father, hallowed be Your name. Your kingdom come. Give us each day our daily bread. And forgive us our sins, for we ourselves also forgive everyone who is indebted to us. And lead us not into temptation.'"

LUKE 11:2-4

Come with me to the New Testament, where we see this same picture unfold in Jesus' ministry. We can gain fresh insight from two specific instances that show the holy gap that often exists between our human requests and His answers.

Turn in your Bible to Luke 11:11-13 first, and then John 4:7-10. Read each short passage, and then meet me back here. For each one, write down a general overview about the difference between (1) what the person wanted or was discussing and (2) what Jesus offered.

• Luke 11:11-13

• John 4:7-10

LUKE 11. Jesus here was talking with His beloved friends about the value and nature and purpose of prayer. As the chapter opens, we see Jesus Himself praying—Son to Father—which must always have fascinated these closest followers of His. On this particular day, it inspired them to ask Him, "Lord, teach us to pray" (v. 1), which He answered by giving them the model of what we now call the Lord's Prayer (vv. 2-4).

But watch this. In verses 11-13 that you just read, He likened prayer to a child asking his or her father for something. For something good. A fish, an egg, a piece of bread, something nice to eat. The last thing any good father is going to do with that request, He said, is to give his child a snake, a scorpion, something that would harm his son or daughter and mock the request made of him. In comparison, God is not just a *good* Father; He is a perfect one. And if we would trust a good earthly father to give good gifts, how much more should we trust our heavenly Father to give us gifts that are even more incredible, even if they don't show up in the package we expected. He loves His children so much—that's you!— that He gives us even more than what's merely good. He gives us what reflects His perfection. He gives us the ultimate gift—*Himself*—the full expression and experience of His Spirit operating within our lives.

God is not just a *good* Father; He is a perfect one.

#ElijahBibleStudy

What did Jesus surprisingly say His heavenly Father would give to those who ask for a temporary want?

JOHN 4. The woman at the well. All she wanted was to dip her bucket in the well, take her water, and go home, back to her secret life and the shame she continually endured. But Jesus, who in breaking with all customs of the day had asked her (a Samaritan woman) for a drink, said there was more He wanted to give her, and that He was there to offer it to her.

Compare Jesus' language in verse 10 with John 7:38-39. What did He mean by saying He could give her "living water"?

Jesus answered and said to her, "If you knew the gift of God, and who it is who says to you, 'Give Me a drink,' you would have asked Him, and He would have given you living water."

JOHN 4:10

Sometimes our deepest desire does not truly reflect our deepest need.

#ElijahBibleStudy

Sometimes, in the moment of drought, we can often assume that our deepest physical desire is an accurate reflection of our truest need. But what *God* wants to give us—the Holy Spirit, along with all the power and abundance of life His Spirit offers—is the ultimate answer. We ask Him for bread, for money, for a husband, for a child. And He may give us those things. He is that kind of Father. But sometimes we are so fixated on our thirst that we are blind to how our requests may be shortsighted and shortchanging. We want rain. Mere water. And given the severity and length of whatever drought we've faced, that's an understandable request. But before that, He wants to give us something else. Something more. Someone living.

A fresh revelation and experience of His Spirit.

His fire.

This is what you really want. I promise you it is.

This week, Father, I invite You—I appeal to You—to adjust my desires until they line up with Yours. Thank You for inviting me to make my requests known to You. But I repent for times when I have not trusted You to answer me in Your sovereign way and in Your sovereign timing. Cultivate in me an overwhelming, unshakable desire for Your holy fire above and before all other desires. Let the skies over Mount Carmel rise above me these next two weeks like a mirror, reflecting back to me the climate of my own soul. Work inside this heart, I pray, until every want of mine is consumed in wanting You, in wanting what I really need. More than anything, amen.

NO MORE HOPSCOTCH

"Then Elijah approached all the people and said, 'How long will you waver between two opinions? If the Lord is God, follow him. But if Baal, follow him.' But the people didn't answer him a word."

1 KINGS 18:21, CSB

Sometimes a single question or statement, inserted at just the right instant, can halt and hush all other conversation. Suddenly there's nothing more to say.

Perhaps the most classic, on-target example is Jesus' comeback to the self-righteous scribes and Pharisees who'd hauled before Him the half-dressed woman caught in the act of adultery, their fists already clenched around the jagged-edged stones of immediate, high-noon judgment. *The law says she DIES for this! Isn't that RIGHT, Jesus?*

You remember the drama of that unforgettable scene—Jesus stooping to the ground, running His finger through the dust, while they loudly, fiendishly badgered Him for a response. After hearing enough of it, He "straightened up" (John 8:7), the Bible says, positioning His influence directly between the mob and the accused woman. Then, letting the intensity of His eyes drill this next sentiment into their hearts, he said, "He who is without sin among you, let him be the first to throw a stone at her."

Mic drop.

All chattering stopped. All the rocks dropped. Dumbstruck, those who'd been spitting epithets only a moment before began silently, one by one, slinking away.

And that's what Elijah did at this pivotal moment on the crest of Mount Carmel. High stakes and high tension were thick in the early morning air. Nearly a thousand pagan prophets had gathered in attendance, along with the entire assembled nation of Israel. It was setting up to be an all-out spiritual throw down. And into this hive of energy and anticipation, Elijah lobbed an all-or-nothing question, right there into the center of his countrymen—a question that we all are required to answer as well.

"How much longer will you waver, hobbling between two opinions?"

1 KINGS 18:21, NLT

Varying translations of this verse give us unique ways of registering our own personal stance on it. As you look at them below, how does each highlighted synonym challenge you in a different, more nuanced way in terms of your one hundred percent commitment level to the one true God?

- In what ways are you "wavering" (NIV) in your allegiance to Him?

- How are you "hesitating" (HCSB) to fully commit or submit to Him?

- In what ways are you "limping" (ESV) along, unsteady, imbalanced?

- What about "halting" (KJV)—stopping and starting, not able to move straight ahead?

Elijah's question is so important and foundational to what this whole episode on the mountain is meant to communicate that I'm settling in on this verse today and tomorrow to allow extra opportunity for self-examination. So pause just a moment before moving on.

Ask the Holy Spirit to let this singular question expose any other unrecognized areas of your life where you're "hobbling" along in your loyalty and devotion to God. Perhaps you're prioritizing other people or activities over Him, even lining them up as equals to Him. Perhaps you're allowing your loyalty to shift back and forth between Him and other allegiances depending on your mood or the pressure from your peers.

Let Elijah's question penetrate the depths of your soul in this moment.

HOW LONG WILL YOU WAVER BETWEEN TWO OPINIONS?

One way to begin determining where your allegiances truly lie is to survey where you commit the bulk of your resources—your time, your money, your words, your talents. (Think of call or text logs, your social media threads, your bank account, etc.) What does a quick, one-month scroll through these databases reveal about your consistency in being loyal to God's claim on your heart and life? I've left plenty of space here for you to reflect and journal.

_____

_____

_____

_____

_____

_____

_____

_____

_____

_____

_____

_____

_____

_____

_____

_____

The original Hebrew word that translates to the English word "waver" is *pacach* (pronounced "paw-SAKH"), a verb meaning "to pass over, spring over, to skip."[1] Think of it as a light-footed bounce, a step that's rarely steady and firm. Or picture it as an old-fashioned game of hopscotch (hop, skip, jump).

The same original word is used in Exodus 12. Read the verse in the margin, which references God's dealings with His people on the eve of their deliverance from Egypt. See if you can detect the phrase that is rendered from this same word. Circle it when you see it. (It's only in there once.)

Pacach was certainly an apt description of the unstable stance of Israel's people during Elijah's lifetime. Though Jezebel had worked hard to eradicate the worship of Yahweh altogether, the people simply possessed too much history with the Lord to abandon their affiliation to Him entirely. They knew what they *should* do. They knew where their spiritual allegiances *should* lie. But they were conflicted. They'd set their worship of Baal beside their worship of God. Like commuter trains running on twin tracks, their loyalties were divided: one leg of faith here, another leg of faith there, hopping back and forth as convenience and cultural pressures dictated.

Because of the spiritual corruption and weakness in Ahab's (and Jezebel's) leadership, the people of Israel believed they were in a bind. They felt that they needed to show at least outward honor to Baal if they hoped to placate their pagan rulers and fly under the radar of governmental judgment.

But Elijah—Yahweh's spokesperson and representative—would not allow for this marginal, watered-down allegiance to continue. He insisted on a clear, exclusive, unadulterated choice.

"HOW LONG WILL YOU WAVER . . . IF THE LORD IS GOD, FOLLOW HIM. BUT IF BAAL, FOLLOW HIM."

One commentator calls Elijah's statement a "dramatized form of the first commandment."[2] Turn to Exodus 20:3 to remind yourself of what this commandment entails. How does Elijah's question mirror this primary law?

It's also akin to a question that Joshua posed during another phase of Israel's journey. Turn to Joshua 24:15, and write it verbatim below.

Joshua's "choose for yourselves today" declaration is surely among the most well-known appeals to loyalty in the Bible. But there are others. Explore these passages and make notes beside the references, summarizing what Moses, Paul, and Jesus were demanding God's people to choose between.

- Deuteronomy 30:15-20
- Matthew 6:24
- Galatians 6:14
- Revelation 3:15

Each of these statements and questions makes clear that a person's choice to play spiritual hopscotch—dancing from one side to the other, attempting to balance the weight of their loyalty equally between the true God and an illegitimate one—is actually an annulment of that loyalty altogether. Ray Pritchard, author of *Fire and Rain*, an exploration on the life of Elijah, calls it "spiritual juggling"—this pressure of trying to stay in the good graces of everyone on all sides, of our God and of our idols. The dance of playing both ends against the middle, hedging our bets to see which side will give us the best bang for our investment, results in a life where we "can't decide who we're going to play for," where we "struggle about which uniform we're going to put on in the morning."[3]

This kind of disjointed lifestyle keeps us off-balance. When we refuse to let other, idolatrous allegiances fall away, we're left to trip through life, limping along, tossed around by worldly philosophies and misguided patterns of thinking, overwhelmed by hardships that are too much for anyone to walk through without holding tightly to God's hand. Worse, we negate our access to His choicest blessings—the sense of His nearness, the fire of His empowering—reserved only for those who choose to seat Him by Himself on the throne of their lives. Yahweh must be God alone to us, or He is not our God at all.

Yahweh must be God alone to us, or He is not our God at all.

#ElijahBibleStudy

Half obedience to God is actually complete disobedience.

#ElijahBibleStudy

The truth is, half obedience to God is actually complete disobedience. "He who is not with Me is against Me," Jesus said (Matt. 12:30), soon after stating the spiritual truism that a "house divided against itself will not stand" (v. 25). Whatever gray areas may exist in the navigation of our lives, there's nothing but darkness and light in this foundational choice that God and His Word lay out before us. Decide. Take your stand—"with Me" or "against Me."

Make your own personal observations about the following questions, and then prepare to discuss them with your group:

1. What makes being a nominal, tepid follower of Jesus more convenient and acceptable in today's culture?

2. What are some of the dynamics and attitudes emerging in current society that could make it even more difficult for young men and women in future generations to remain unmoved in their allegiance to God?

No more hopscotching. Today is the day of decision. No more riding the fence. No more dancing between allegiances. No more caving to fear or outside pressure. You are a fierce woman of God, with an opportunity to experience—like Elijah did—the stability of being anchored in solid, single-minded devotion to Him. Put aside all other loves (we'll be talking throughout the rest of the week about how to do that) and recommit yourself to the one true God of Abraham, Isaac, and Jacob. The God who answers by fire.

The conviction you may feel after studying through these Scriptures today is God's Spirit at work in your heart. It is actually the sting and burn from that fire falling from heaven, exposing and consuming the illegitimate idols in your life. Don't resist its heat. Don't move away from it to a safer place. Confess what He exposes and let Him do away with those cheapened compromises that lead you to satisfy your desires in godless, unsatisfying places. Let Him be first. Let Him be all. He is always enough.

SAY SOMETHING

"Alas, O Lord, the great and awesome God, who keeps His covenant and lovingkindness for those who love Him and keep His commandments, we have sinned, committed iniquity, acted wickedly and rebelled . . ."

DANIEL 9:4b-5

The Old Testament prophets expected to get a response. They didn't talk just to be heard. The word of the Lord was intended to come back in the form of repentant hearts and contrite responses.

Like when the Lord sent the prophet Nathan to confront a cover-up in the house of David. He delivered a parable to the king about a rich man who, though flush with flocks and herds, chose to rob his neighbors of the lone sheep in their pasture, simply because he decided he wanted it. David, too deep in denial over his adultery with Bathsheba and his tacit role in the killing of her husband, missed the subtle analogy. Instead, pulling from the predictable playbook of self-delusion, he ranted to Nathan against the selfish injustice of this proverbial rich man's brazen deed.

Seeing that the roundabout approach hadn't worked, Nathan opted to go the more direct route. "You are the man!" (2 Sam. 12:7). *Don't you see, David? YOU are the rich man who stole everything his neighbor ever had.* Couldn't be more prophetically clear than that.

Checkmate.

King David hung his head, mulling his options. Anger? Throw this man out? Or worse, say nothing. Ignore the charge. Remain silent. Feign ignorance. Shrug his shoulders with indifference. "What are you talking about?" But instead of these options, his lips formed the repentant words that tell us David was a different kind of man: "I have sinned against the LORD" (v. 13). Exactly what Nathan's rebuke had been intended to produce.

And it's exactly what Elijah's was intended to produce as well.

> "Elijah approached all the people and said, 'How long will you waver between two opinions? If the LORD is God, follow him. But if Baal, follow him.' But the people didn't answer him a word."
>
> 1 KINGS 18:21, CSB

Revisit the verse we studied yesterday, which appears here in the margin. What did the biblical historian of 1 Kings report about how the people responded to Elijah's question?

Deafening silence. Icy stillness. Elijah had drawn this line in the sand—"If the LORD is God, follow him. But if Baal, follow him"—and the people said nothing. Not one of them spoke up.

But of course their wordlessness was indeed a loud and clear response. It revealed their apathy, their indifference, their complacency, their overall cluelessness. By saying nothing, they were really saying everything—that their hearts were unstable, their loyalties divided, their minds unmade. They were complicit in the nation's pervasive godlessness by their own silence in regard to it. And apparently, until challenged by Elijah that morning, they'd fully and unthinkingly intended to keep riding out this balancing act for the rest of their lives.

Where would you say your life gives silent assent to habits or practices that you know are out of line with absolute devotion to God?

What makes saying nothing feel like a more acceptable option than speaking up?

If one of your coworkers or closest friends was asked to describe your allegiance to God, which adjective might that person use?

○ Nominal ○ Obvious
○ Bold ○ Quiet
○ Complete ○ Dogmatic
○ Indifferent ○ Weak

Explain your reasons for selecting that word?

Are you satisfied with the adjective you chose? Why or why not?

Now turn your attention inward. How do you sense God's Spirit pricking your heart about cementing your allegiance to Him until it's absolutely unmistakable to everyone around who knows you?

The real danger of our disloyalty to God, whether active or passive, actually goes much deeper than merely the making of a spiritual choice. It's not just a decision with spiritual implications; it's a whole way of life decision.

In ancient Israel, where syncretism ran rampant, exclusive allegiance to Yahweh meant living with a perspective on society that was completely unlike that which the followers of Baal embraced. In a God-centered worldview, when properly understood, all people are equal in relationship to one another, no matter their social status, all equally valuable to one divine King. This is what they and their ancestors had been taught. Yahweh was viewed as the owner of the land and the ultimate leader of the people. *All* the people.

Remember what *syncretism* means? We talked about it briefly in Week One. It's the acceptance and blending of different religious beliefs or practices, creating an ungrounded tolerance for all faith positions, as opposed to upholding the truth as being true no matter what.

But the followers of Baal saw things differently. Their god legitimized a hierarchical structure and stratification where the king, along with an elite ruling class of the successful, influential, and wealthy, were ascribed with having greater divine connectivity and favor from the gods. Their success was a sign of the gods' approval.

So Elijah's ultimatum to Israel, as one writer surmises, "was not merely which God to serve, but in what social configuration to live in." It meant "enduring the consequences of that choice both economically and socially."[4] In other words, Elijah was asking them to make a decision that would impact every area of their lives, how they navigated their view of others, and how they viewed their own personal success. This ultimatum concerning which God or god they intended to serve would in effect determine their entire worldview.

> **Consider the implications of the last several paragraphs. Underline any portions that you see demonstrated or abused in modern-day culture.**

> **Now consider it personally. Use the space in the margin to record how a biblical view of God impacts how you live and the decisions you make in areas such as:**

> - **Finances**
> - **Marriage**
> - **Occupation**
> - **Recreation**

> - **Parenting**
> - **Friendships**
> - **Civil rights**
> - **Political views**

> **(Discuss two or three of these with a friend you can trust.)**

In time, this refusal to secure their allegiances would cost the Northern Kingdom of Israel their existence. Twelve evil kings or so after Ahab, after generations of following "worthless idols"—until, as Scripture says, the people became "worthless themselves" (2 Kings 17:15, CSB)—Samaria fell to the Assyrians. "The LORD removed Israel from his presence just as he had declared through all his servants the prophets" (v. 23)—all those prophets who, like Elijah, had sought from God's people an answer, an acknowledgment of their sinful duplicity, one that would stick for more than a day and a half, one that would lead to a permanent change from this repeated pattern.

Turn to 2 Kings 17:35-39 and review the commandments and instructions that God had given His people. Make notes in the margin.

Yet note in verse 41 the summary statement against them:

• They feared and worshiped _____.
• But they also _____ their _____.

For a little additional study on the heart of God for His people and what He was eagerly willing to do for them if they stepped up and admitted the fallacy of their idol-loving ways, turn to Judges 10. Write a short summary answer to the following questions about this passage.

Verse 6: What had their pattern again become?

Verse 7: How did God respond to it?

Verses 8-9: What did it cost the people?

Verse 10: How did they respond in their distress?

Verses 11-14: What did God say to them at first?

Verse 15: How did the people answer Him?

Verse 16a: What did they actively do?

Verse 16b: How did God respond now?

Let me tell you something. "The eyes of the LORD are toward the righteous and His ears are open to their cry" (Ps. 34:15). Sure, His face is set "against evildoers" (v. 16). Those who continue opposing Him, resisting Him, and refusing to respond to His calls for repentance are revealing by their actions and attitudes that they have not surrendered their will to His. They have set themselves against the desires of God for their lives.

But that is not you, my sister, or else your heart wouldn't be quivering right now with a holy eagerness to fly back into His arms with everything you're made of.

> "*The righteous* cry, and the LORD hears and delivers them out of all their troubles. The LORD is near to the brokenhearted and saves those who are crushed in spirit."

PSALM 34:17-18

Picture yourself with me right now. Sunrise atop Mount Carmel. Hear the words of Elijah echoing off the surrounding cliff formations and cascading down into the valley. As his final syllable fades out of listening range, experience the silence, descending over the whole crowd. Feel its heartbeat. Ache from it. And while everyone else around you warily shifts their weight from one foot to the other, be the one who's unwilling to choke down the cry of loyalty to Yahweh that is outsizing your capacity for holding it in. Even if all the rest stand silent, turn your voice into a chorus of one.

The people didn't answer him a word?

Not us. Not you and me. Not *these* two people.

Together, let's confess the words of the prophet Jeremiah. Why not say them out loud, right now?

> "We know our wickedness, O LORD, the iniquity of our fathers, for we have sinned against You. Do not despise us, for Your own name's sake; do not disgrace the throne of Your glory; remember and do not annul Your covenant with us. Are there any among the idols of the nations who give rain? Or can the heavens grant showers? Is it not You, O LORD our God? Therefore we hope in You, for You are the one who has done all these things."

JEREMIAH 14:20-22

Amen. Yes, *amen.*

DAY FOUR

YOU FIRST

"A person's pride will humble him,
but a humble spirit will gain honor."

PROVERBS 29:23, CSB

I admire confidence in other people. Especially the strong, understated type. These kinds of folks don't have to say it; you see it. The quiet humility of their actions speaks louder than any pompous words ever could—a visible willingness to defer to others and deflect attention. They're not pushovers. Far from it. They just know who they are—they know Who they belong to—they know the power that is theirs because of that relationship.

And they know Who can send the fire.

For me personally, when I see modern-day Elijahs standing securely in the face of overwhelming life challenges, or even just a daily dilemma, all while maintaining a sense of peace and decorum, even a measure of joy, I am convicted and inspired. Despite all they're facing, they have no doubt they're on the winning side. And even as they navigate and pains-takingly negotiate their daily realities, they carry a steady assurance that remains with them and emanates through them.

Like the Old Testament prophet Elijah. He knew he was on the winning side. He felt no need to vie for attention or compete for first place. He was thankful and trusting that Yahweh had his back. This steely confidence is actually one of the main things that first attracted me to Elijah, and it compelled me to want to study his life and emulate his example.

> Start today's lesson by reading the following section from our key passage this week (1 Kings 18). It's printed for you on the next page. Here, Elijah was laying out the terms of the contest to all those gathered on Mount Carmel: Israel on one side; the pagan prophets on the other. Underline all the portions that display Elijah's *confidence*.

"'Let two bulls be given to us. They are to choose one bull for themselves, cut it in pieces, and place it on the wood but not light the fire. I will prepare the other bull and place it on the wood but not light the fire. Then you call on the name of your god, and I will call on the name of the LORD. The God who answers with fire, he is God.'

All the people answered, 'That's fine.'

Then Elijah said to the prophets of Baal, 'Since you are so numerous, choose for yourselves one bull and prepare it first. Then call on the name of your god but don't light the fire.'"

1 KINGS 18:23-25, CSB

After all the people agreed to the terms of the contest, what did Elijah allow the Baalists to do?

What reason did he give for it?

Turn your attention inward now for some self-evaluation. Write a few sentences to describe how you normally react (emotionally, physically) when you feel outnumbered or overwhelmed in some area of your life, especially when the stakes of what you're up against are particularly high.

Now use the margin space to prayerfully expound on your answer:

- How do you react to or treat the other people who are involved in those kinds of situations?
- How do you feel about yourself at those times?
- In situations like these, is it easy or fairly difficult for you to let others go first or take primary positioning?
- What do you think you'll lose if you defer to them?
- What does your reaction say about the state of your heart? About your confidence in the Lord?

Even though there were other Israelites on Mount Carmel that day, Elijah was the only one who was unapologetic and verbal about his complete allegiance to Yahweh. He was, in essence, outnumbered 850 to 1. He certainly felt that way. "I am the only remaining prophet of the LORD," he said (1 Kings 18:22, CSB). Despite this, he willingly deferred to his adversaries in this contest, allowing them the first opportunity to invoke the fiery response of their god.

The question is: *Why?*—why would he do this? and *How?*—how could he muster up the courage and confidence to do it? With such grand odds at stake and in such a highly intimidating environment, how could he show no signs of concern or worry or insecurity, even while giving his opponents the seeming advantage of going first?

It's because of something he knew—and I mean *really* knew—and it's the one thing I want you to walk away from today's devotional believing and consistently incorporating into your reactions toward the overwhelming circumstances in your life. Here it is:

THE PERCEIVED ADVANTAGE OF BEING FIRST IS ALWAYS TRUMPED BY THE ACTUAL ADVANTAGE OF HAVING ACCESS TO GOD'S FIRE.

When you know that God is *for* you, when you know His Spirit lives within you, and when you're convinced (as the gospel says you can be) that His favor and presence rests upon you, you are no longer consumed with insecurity about the odds that may be stacked against you. Neither the "best" nor the "biggest" nor the "first" is any comparison for having God's blessing and backing.

So the real question becomes this:

DO YOU BELIEVE THAT YOUR GOD IS THE ONE TRUE GOD OR NOT?

Elijah knew the only fire that was going to fall that day would be coming from Yahweh's hand. He *knew* it. That's why an absolute confidence could brim within his heart. His willingness to wait, defer, and lead from a position of humility communicated the assurance of his conviction. He basically said, "You take first; I'll take fire."

> When you know that God is *for* you, that His Spirit lives within you, and that His favor and presence are upon you, you are no longer consumed with insecurity about the odds that may be stacked against you.
>
> #ElijahBibleStudy

Skim back through the previous couple of paragraphs and, if you didn't already, highlight or underline any portions that bring to mind and resonate with circumstances you're facing in your life right now. Pause and ask the Holy Spirit to speak to you in regard to what He's showing you.

Think back over the last few days. Evaluate what your recent actions, attitudes, and responses to others have been reflecting about your *confidence* in God (or lack thereof) to fight for you, protect you, and pave the way for you?

Use the chart below to record some of your specific behaviors and what they reveal. I've given you an example from my own life to start.

BEHAVIOR	WHY?
Sometimes I insert myself into a conversation.	I don't fully trust God to make room for me.

This principle we're studying today—about having confidence in God, despite being outnumbered or overwhelmed—can be seen in many different scenarios throughout the Scriptures.

For example, Goliath was much bigger than David, but David had God on his side. "You come to me with a sword and with a spear and with a javelin, but I come to you in the name of the LORD of hosts, the God of the armies of Israel" (1 Sam. 17:45, ESV). Joseph was outnumbered and overpowered by his big brothers, and yet God's favor and blessing rested on him as the younger brother, so that even when they planned and executed evil against Him, God turned it around "for good" (Gen. 50:20).

What other biblical examples come to your mind that underscore this principle? (I've listed a few in the margin to spur your thinking.) Why do you think God would make this theme so prevalent and repeated in Scripture?

- Joshua against Jericho (Josh. 6:1-5)

- Samson against the Philistines (Judg. 16:21-30)

Take a peek at one of my favorite Old Testament examples, Judges 7:2-9, which chronicles the famed beginnings of Gideon's battle against one hundred forty thousand Midianite soldiers.

- Nehemiah against his opponents (Neh. 6:1-9)

- Verse 2: How did the Lord describe Gideon's original army?

- Paul against a storm at sea (Acts 27:18-25)

- Verses 3-8: Do the math. How many men did Gideon start with? How many did he end up sending home? How many remained to go into battle?

- Verse 9: What was Yahweh's promise to Gideon and his small army?

My favorite portion of this passage is found in that second verse, when God said to Gideon, "The people who are with you are too many for Me to give Midian into their hands" (v. 2). In other words, the more resources Gideon had at his disposal, the less of a victory he would experience. Having more was actually working against him.

Did you catch what I said? Having more worked *against* him!

I'm floored by this. I often wonder how many times I've refused to release things from my life that, at the time, seemed advantageous or even necessary. In hindsight though, I realize they were actually acting as repellents to the fire of heaven that God wanted to give. I continually try to remember what God told Gideon to do: "I will deliver you with the 300 men . . . so let all the other people go" (v. 7). Translation? Don't be afraid to have fewer. Don't be afraid to go second. Don't be afraid to look weaker by comparison. *I've got your back, and you've got My favor.* That's all you need on your side to secure the victory.

That's where Gideon got his confidence. Where Elijah got his confidence. Where you and I can get our confidence too. And when we're confident—with that kind of confidence—we don't need to gather more reinforcements, or go first, or maneuver ourselves into a favorable position for outsmarting and outperforming everybody else. Instead we can walk into any situation with authentic *humility*, which is one of the key elements that invites the fire of heaven.

Our flesh is so easily tickled toward pride and self-sufficiency that we instinctively lean toward wanting to be first, to be the best, to have the most. So God, in order to curb this tendency of ours, often allows us to enter situations where the odds are tilted against us, where we're liable to experience a frightful twinge of insufficiency. But rather than avoid these moments, be like Elijah—embrace them as an opportunity to practice humility, to defer to others, and to refuse succumbing to insecurity.

Don't back down and run away from hard things. Believe instead that God can do unbelievable things in the face of them.

> One of the keys that invites the fire of heaven in our lives is

> _____.

> "Humble yourselves in the presence of the Lord, and He will exalt you."
>
> JAMES 4:10

As you close today's lesson, read the following verses slowly and out loud. Choose one to write on a 3x5 card and post where you will see it regularly throughout the next week. Ask the Lord to cement its truths into your heart. Then ask Him to help you be able to react, respond, and relate to others with a greater sense of confidence in who He is and what He can accomplish on your behalf.

- Psalm 73:23-26
- 2 Corinthians 3:4-5

STOP THE FRENZY

"When you pray, do not keep on babbling like pagans, for they think they will be heard because of their many words."

MATTHEW 6:7, NIV

If I could choose only one word to describe how the majority of people in our current culture feel on a routine, daily basis, it would be *exhausted*. Next time you ask someone "How are you doing?" and if you're willing to hang around after they've said, "Fine, thank you," *exhaustion* is most likely what you'll hear next.

We're so busy. We're so stretched. The rat race has swallowed us whole. We're overwhelmed at the thought of what we already know is coming up in the day ahead of us, before we've factored in the stuff that we don't even yet know to expect. The constant clawing to accomplish and succeed, to garner attention and accolade, has made this society a weary one to live in.

So our relationship with God, which is the defining treasure in our lives—not just in theory but in everyday, practical living—should help us deal with this ragged, runaway exhaustion we can easily feel. And it should distinguish the pace and pursuits of our lives from those who are unbelieving.

The truths of Scripture, with its requirement of Sabbath rest and margin, with its encouragement to abandon all worry in favor of prayerful trust, with its promise of peace that peaks all levels of human comprehension—should keep us sane and settled amid a seriously over-scheduled, achievement-oriented world.

On Mount Carmel, in the ongoing saga of Elijah against the prophets of Baal on Mount Carmel, the pagans took the first opportunity to prove the power of the god they served. And their turn would be marked by the same insane exhaustion that we see marking many of our lives today.

Turn back to 1 Kings 18:23-24 where Elijah gave instructions about how the day's proceedings were going to go. Make a list of the four things that each opponent was supposed to do in preparation for the showdown.

1. Choose _____ for the sacrifice
2. _____ it up into pieces
3. Place it on the _____
4. Call on _____

What was each participant told *not* to do?

According to verse 24, how would the winner be determined?

The God/god who _____ is _____.

Let the games begin.

And now, sit back, relax, and observe the way of pagans—the exhausting methods of those who have no security or confidence in their god and are not able to rest in the knowledge of receiving faithful, loving oversight and care. Notice the difference between Elijah and the idol worshipers in two broad categories: (1) the *time* they invested and (2) the *temperament* they demonstrated.

TIME

"Then they took the ox which was given them and they prepared it and called on the name of Baal from morning until noon . . ."

1 KINGS 18:26a

The first part of the morning was taken up with preparing the sacrifice, followed by the beginning of their various rituals for arousing the attention of their god. Remember there were more than eight hundred prophets involved in the ceremony—four hundred fifty prophets of Baal and four hundred prophets of Baal's female consort, Asherah.

According to the verse in the margin, how long did this activity go on?

They were surely disappointed that Baal was taking so long to respond. But by the time the sun had centered itself in the sky, they were sure it wouldn't be long now. In their convoluted theology, Baal was the god of the sun. In fact, they thought him to be god of the entirety of nature. Surely now that his great, burning presence was directly above them, they believed he was right on the doorstep of igniting the kindling of their sacrifice with his divine power. If he was capable of doing anything, he could certainly—easily!—cause fire to come blazing out of the heavens like a lightning bolt.

So they heightened their antics to capitalize on their supposed midday advantage. Their attempts at garnering the attention of their idol can only be described as an extended period of mass hysteria and chaos. As each hour passed, they escalated the frenzied madness.

Underline the last sentence in the previous paragraph.

What does this next verse tell us about how much longer they continued imploring Baal to act? ⎯⎯⎯⎯⎯⎯⎯→ "When midday was past, they raved until the time of the offering of the evening sacrifice."

1 KINGS 18:29a

Looks like this was turning into an all-day event. And as the sun went down, their level of angst, fear, and wild-eyed desperation went up.

TEMPERAMENT

The time element stirred the mania in their temperament.

Scan verses 26-29 and write down some of the phrases the Bible uses to describe the fervor of their religious display.

There seemed to be no end to the frenzied, frantic, frenetic madness of their supplications. They pleaded hysterically for a reciprocal response, fully expecting their fast-paced gyrations and fancy footwork to attract something spectacular from heaven. Their long, stringy hair dripped with sweat from their exhausting exertions, even as they abused their bodies and cut themselves with knives until blood gushed from their filleted, self-inflicted wounds—whatever it took to impress Baal with the depth of their devotion. "When they danced," Ray Pritchard writes, "they would scream and beat their drums and lower their bodies almost to the ground. Sexual immorality lay at the core of Baal worship. [So there was] wild screaming and various sexual antics up on the mountain" as well.[5]

All the noise. The shrieking. The running around and throwing themselves down. Yet it was all to no avail. It generated no response from above. "No voice, no one answered, no one paid attention" (v. 29).

Meanwhile, Elijah and the rest of the people of Israel waited for this chaotic scene to wind down. Elijah even, in a truly humorous moment from Scripture, taunted the pagan revelers from his seat at the picnic table, wondering what could be holding up their precious god from paying them any mind.

It's really hilarious to read and imagine his verbal jabs inflaming them even more.

The important task for us, more than trying to interpret the wildness of their behavior, is to make sure that our own behavior doesn't mirror it. Since we are *not* idol worshipers and do not serve an impotent god, our spiritual lives should not be marked by the same exhausting realities that mark theirs. During periods of waiting that stretch out much longer than we'd prefer, our confidence should not be permanently shaken. Instead, like the psalmist, our declaration should be: "I would have despaired unless I had believed that I would see the goodness of the LORD" (Ps. 27:13).

Recall with me the main question that you and I have been pondering all this week: "How long will you waver between two opinions?" Hopefully you remember the Hebrew word for it—*pacach.*

> **Think back (or look back to page 125) to recall the meaning of this word. Record some of the English synonyms that describe its meaning.**

"At noon Elijah mocked them, saying, 'Cry aloud, for he is a god. Either he is musing, or he is relieving himself, or he is on a journey, or perhaps he is asleep and must be awakened.'"

1 KINGS 18:27, ESV

Now look carefully again at how the last line of 1 Kings 18:26 characterizes the idolaters' activity. Notice that the whole idea in the original text is from the same word: *pacach*. Do you see it? All that bouncing around, leaping from one stance to the next. It's the same kind of exhausting, back-and-forth "wavering." It comes from the same root system.

Before reading further, what conclusions might you draw from the significance of this word being used to compare what Israel was doing in their spiritual allegiance and what the false prophets were doing in their false worship?

What Elijah was challenging Israel to resist in verse 21—the exhausting, "wavering," hopping between one loyalty and another, between their allegiance to God and to something other than God—is precisely how the Baalists' worship is described. *Pacach.* The draining, taxing, fatiguing hard work that depicts the existence of those who worship idols was not to be mirrored in the experience of God's people.

A frenzied life is not a faith-filled life.

Whether it's God's people not staying firmly tied to Him, or godless people tying their hopes to godless pursuits, it invariably leads to an empty, hollow, unsatisfying conclusion, even after all that time and energy, after all that work and effort.

Oh, the heartbreaking emptiness of serving a god who not only *won't* respond but *can't*. Every idol we place our trust in—whether entertainment or achievement or relationships or connections or anything else that we expect to satisfy us with meaning and fulfillment—they are all incapable of it. They are all phony gods, and seeking to garner satisfaction from them will leave us exhausted.

And so the only percentage of the population who should be living in continual weariness and exhaustion should be those who refuse to cement their loyalties in the one true God. We, however, whose God has given us His Son, who has declared us His own beloved children, and who has demonstrated His utter willingness and capacity to give us everything we need—beyond what we could ask or think—we should

A frenzied life is not a faith-filled life.

#ElijahBibleStudy

be able to rest and enjoy a sense of inner (and external) contentment in every situation.

He doesn't need impressing. And *we* don't need the kind of exhausted existence that a life in step with Him is designed to free us from.

> **In what areas of your life are you most exhausted as you try to get something or someone to satisfy you?**

> **What most exhausts you about trying to appease and gain their approval?**

> **Turn to one or more of the following passages, and jot down beside each reference a principle to be gleaned from what it tells you.**
>
> • Psalm 135:15-18
>
> • Isaiah 44:9-11
>
> • Habakkuk 2:18-20

And now, for just a moment as we reach the end of another full week, let's sit still with these thoughts for the last few minutes. The counterfeits on Carmel and in our own hearts have been exposed, and we've begun to purge the misguided, illegitimate desires embedded in our own souls. Flip back through the last four or five lessons to remind yourself of what God's Spirit has been showing you and teaching you since the week started.

Below, write down one takeaway from each lesson that the Holy Spirit has highlighted for you personally.

Day One: Rain and Fire

Day Two: No More Hopscotch

Day Three: Say Something

Day Four: You First

Day Five: Stop the Frenzy

You have not been called to an exhausting spiritual life—wavering, weaving, overworking, selfishly wanting. You are His beloved daughter. Heir to a great inheritance. You can live in settled confidence. You can adjust from folly to faith. You can apply the hard-learned lessons of the process and rest in His sure provision.

And you can know the fire is sure to come.

> Confess to your Father any of the ways that you recognize your own life in the example of the idol worshipers on Carmel. Repent of the areas where you've stopped trusting Him, trading faith for doubt, panic, and fear. Then ask His Spirit to empower you to live in a way that's clearly distinct from those who do not know Him, as He reminds you of the favor and approval you can already claim because of your relationship with God through Jesus Christ. Ask Him to teach you to rest and live in step with the rhythm of grace.

"Truly my soul finds rest in God; my salvation comes from him. Truly he is my rock and my salvation; he is my fortress, I will never be shaken."

PSALM 62:1-2, NIV

Carmel

EXPERIENCING THE AUTHENTIC

FIRE: SUBMITTING TO GOD'S POWER

#ELIJAHBIBLESTUDY

WEEK FIVE

INVITING THE FIRE

HOW TO INVITE THE FIRE OF GOD

1. Be _____.

Elijah _____ the altar.

He _____ the promises of God's _____.

He _____ the _____ of Baal.

He _____ his trust in God.

2. Step _____.

Don't only be intentional, but be _____. Live the kind of life that steps forward, out and _____ from the crowd.

3. Never _____ the power of a _____ _____.

Prayer doesn't _____ God. Prayer just _____ all the things He _____ to do for us anyway.

After Elijah prayed that prayer, the sky _____ _____, and God _____ down _____.

Video and audio sessions available for purchase and rent at LifeWay.com/Elijah.

AN INTENTIONAL SACRIFICE

"Therefore, brothers and sisters, in view of the mercies of God, I urge you to present your bodies as a living sacrifice, holy and pleasing to God; this is your true worship."

ROMANS 12:1, CSB

In November 2018, I traveled to Israel and toured the land of the Bible. It wasn't my first time. Nearly twenty years prior, my parents took me with them as part of a group my father was hosting, teaching the stories of Scripture in the land where they first took place. But this most recent trip was the first time I remember visiting Mount Carmel. Being on that mountain was the highlight of the trip for me. After all the months I'd spent focusing on Elijah's story, and knowing I'd soon be writing the study that you're holding in your hands right now, I was mesmerized as I stood atop the mountain overlooking the Jezreel and Kishon Valleys.

At the centerpiece of the memorial grounds stands an oversized statue of Elijah. He's wielding a dagger high above his head in his right hand, while his left foot rests with confident triumph over one of the prophets of Baal. An inscription at the base of the monument alludes to this unforgettable moment in history when the heavens opened above his altar. When the fire fell. My heart burned within me on that day—the same way it's doing right now.

Because, sister, here we are.

In the fifth week of Bible study. With Elijah on Mount Carmel.

See "Digging Deeper III" on page 182. When the fire of God will fall from heaven.

The people of Israel had just finished watching the hours-long, vain efforts of the prophets of Baal, with not even a flicker of fire to show for it. And now, it was Yahweh's turn. Elijah knew for a faith-filled fact that the holy, fiery power of Yahweh would soon fall, and his unmitigated confidence in Him was about to be confirmed and revealed.

But first things first. In the next scene to unfold on the mountain, Elijah painstakingly prepared and presented a sacrifice worthy of receiving God's fire. And we must mark it well, because his deliberate, meticulous actions preceding Yahweh's response would demonstrate to everyone—and to us—the significance of paying attention to the way we offer ourselves to God. Offering our whole lives as a "holy and pleasing" acceptable sacrifice becomes a magnet that invites the favor and blessing of God.

> An extravagant gift may impress people, but an intentional gift is what impresses God.

Turn to 1 Kings 18:30-35. Read it through, and then keep these verses on hand because we'll cover this entire passage today.

Beginning in verse 30, what did Elijah do to "the altar of the LORD" that had been torn down? He _____ it.

After this, he started to rebuild it. What significant feature does verse 31 detail?

What does this element represent?

What reminder would this action have stirred in the hearts and minds of:

• Those who were not followers of Yahweh?

• Those who were part of the nation of Israel?

Take time to consider the fact that Elijah completely avoided anything that was devoted to the worship of Baal, even in part. He preferred instead doing the hard, sweat-producing work of rebuilding an altar where sacrifices had once been made to God, prior to the building of the temple (see 1 Kings 3:2), rather than the ease of using a well-built framework that had been dedicated to idols. To him, the extra effort was worth it.

Equally telling is the fact that Elijah also refused to start from scratch, building something brand new. The prophet's goal was not to introduce a new form of worship but to respect Yahweh's history with His people. But in its dilapidated state, this altar that Elijah chose to use was in no condition to receive God's fire. It needed repair. It needed rebuilding.

And so he rebuilt it with *twelve* stones. Not eleven. Not thirteen. *Twelve*—an important number in the annals of Israel's history. With each stone he laid, Elijah reclaimed and honored Yahweh's ancient promises and brought them forward to this present point in history. Suddenly the stories their grandfathers and great-grandfathers had told them as children reignited in their memories, reanimating their distant imaginations, reminding them of Abraham, Isaac, and Jacob, and the covenant Yahweh had established with them.

The twelve stones symbolized the twelve tribes and would have pointed to the conquest of Canaan, including the allotment of property right here in what was once known as God's glorious promised land. It was spiritual heritage and inheritance all in one, surging through the hearts of a nation who'd forgotten what they were all about—all because of Elijah's thoughtful and intentional choice to select *twelve* scattered stones and wedge them tightly together for the foundation of the altar. His discerning and deliberate actions at this juncture not only emphasized Yahweh's covenant but also reminded them of something more.

> Flip back a few chapters to 1 Kings 12, which follows the death of Solomon. Read verses 15-17, as well as verse 19, and look at what happened to the nation of Israel when Rehoboam (Solomon's son) rejected the people's pleas for reform. Describe the status of Israel from that time forward.

Here on Mount Carmel stood the citizens of Israel who represented the ten tribes of the north. They were still in staunch opposition to the tribes of Judah and Benjamin in the south. This was a divided nation. But as Elijah deliberately formed the base of Yahweh's altar, repairing and rebuilding it with those twelve symbols, Israel symbolically appeared as a cohesive, reconciled unit—the way the Lord had originally intended His people to be.

Given what we've studied so far, write down some of the spiritual implications that Elijah's detailed rebuilding communicated to the people that day about Yahweh's original intent regarding . . .

• Their relationship to Him:

• His covenant with them:

• The importance of their unity:

Before we move any further, take a moment to personalize what you've studied. In what specific ways have you seen modern society disregard or actively deface the "twelve stones" of God's bedrock promises and replace them with other forms of "worship"? How is God compelling you to rebuild these altars in your own sphere of influence?

As you discuss this topic with your group, do so with a heart toward what we as the church can do, both collectively and individually, to intentionally repair and restore what's been lost by getting away from God's foundations.

Elijah's precision and attention to detail continued with another series of deliberate steps, each one proving to be more stunning and surprising than what he'd done at first with the twelve stones.

> **Check back in with 1 Kings 18 now and describe what happened next:**
>
> **Verse 32: What did he create *around* the altar?**
>
>
>
> **Verse 33: What did he arrange *atop* the altar?**
>
>
>
> **Verse 34: What did he pour *over* the altar?**
>
>
>
> **Verse 35: What was the final appearance of the altar?**

Imagine the people's disbelief, having lived every day for the last three years treating each drop of water as a precious commodity, now seeing it sloshed over the altar until it could hold no more. If water was what they'd come to Mount Carmel for, they hadn't come to see it wasted and poured out on the ground!

But nothing was being wasted here. Everything was intentional. The seemingly ridiculous abundance of water—once, twice, three times more unthinkable with each thorough dousing—was intended to underscore the miraculous nature of what was about to occur. It would draw unmistakable recognition to the power and full authority that belonged to God and God alone.

Reread and underline the last line of the previous paragraph. Then, using details from the verse in the margin (1 Kings 18:38), write a few sentences on how Elijah's addition of water contributed to the "unmistakable recognition" of Yahweh's power.

> "Then the fire of the LORD fell and consumed the burnt offering and the wood and the stones and the dust, and licked up the water that was in the trench."
>
> **1 KINGS 18:38**

This divine response is what we want. Our heart's desire is that our whole lives be a worthy offering that produces "a fragrance of Christ to God" (2 Cor. 2:15).

Our offerings to the Lord today are not constituted and composed of such things as oxen, stone altars, and water-filled moats. But as the apostle Paul spelled out plainly in Romans 12:1, we do present ourselves to God as "a living sacrifice"—"holy and pleasing"—as being indicative of our "true worship." The sacrifice is our full, living, breathing selves— our time, our talents, our treasures, our bodies (which are temples of the Holy Spirit). We surrender them each day to Him as instruments for His glory.

But notice Paul didn't just tell us we *must* do it; he told us *how* to do it, in a way that is "holy and pleasing" to God. This kind of total-life offering requires thoughtfulness—a consistent intentionality on our part. It won't happen if we're haphazard or only casually attentive, nor can we offer ourselves begrudgingly or resentfully. Instead, Elijah's example should compel us to examine our own lives today and ask questions like these:

- *Are we conscious and premeditated in honoring our Father with the output of our hours, decisions, priorities, attitudes, and actions, or do we leave it all to chance?*

- *Do we take time to carefully consider how we can create margin for His glory to be glaringly displayed in our lives?*

Because if we are looking for the God of fire to answer by fire, we need to be as diligent as Elijah in preparing the sacrifice to receive it.

For each category below, try accurately estimating where you currently fall on the scale. Obviously your answer could be different next week or next month, as you continue letting God deal with your heart in these matters. But use this exercise to gain a daringly honest perspective on how you're doing it right now. Rate yourself from 1 to 10—with 1 being poor and 10 being excellent.

TIME

How well are you prioritizing your time, making valuable use of it to God? (Do you prioritize the things that are important to Him in your schedule, or do you just hope they'll happen?)

1   2   3   4   5   6   7   8   9   10

Poor   Excellent

Why did you choose this rating?

TALENTS

How faithfully are you using your gifts and abilities to honor God and fulfill your purpose? (Do you reserve your best self for everyone else except the workings of the house of God and encouraging the people of God?)

1   2   3   4   5   6   7   8   9   10

Poor   Excellent

Why did you choose this rating?

TREASURES

How deliberately are you investing your financial resources to enhance the kingdom of God? (Are you committed to the principle of tithes and offerings?)

| 1 | 2 | 3 | 4 | 5 | 6 | 7 | 8 | 9 | 10 |

Poor   Excellent

Why did you choose this rating?

As you allow the Holy Spirit to examine your life and encourage you toward intentionality in these areas, remember that you are a beloved daughter with no need to earn your Father's approval and blessing. You have been saved by faith, not by works. Your relationship with Him is established, and it will endure.

So relax. Presenting yourself to the Lord is an exercise in gratitude. It's something you can sustain, not by tireless effort, but only by walking in step to the rhythm of His grace and depending on the empowerment of His Spirit. Seek Him in prayer and ask for insight on how He wants you to adjust your life to best honor Him. He will give you the clarity, and He will also give you the desire to please Him, "for it is God who is at work in you, both to will and to work for His good pleasure" (Phil. 2:13).

He wants His Spirit to consume you, and for His fruit and gifts to be expressed through you, so that your life becomes a billboard that shows forth the glory of God.

COMPLETELY HIS

"The eyes of the LORD move to and fro throughout the earth that He may strongly support those whose heart is completely His."

2 CHRONICLES 16:9a

Yesterday we saw Elijah's commitment to prepare a worthy sacrifice, but the lessons we learn from his example on Mount Carmel don't stop there.

> **Turn to 1 Kings 18:36. Reading just the opening phrase, how does your Bible describe the action Elijah took after preparing his sacrifice on the altar?**
>
> He _____

Different versions say he "came up" or "walked up" or "came near" or "approached." I like how the New International Version says it: "Elijah stepped forward." Stepped forward and away from the crowd. Stepped up and out on his own. Stepped into a position of leading the people instead of melding seamlessly with them. He created distance between himself and the halfhearted followers of Yahweh, and he directly contradicted the prophets of Baal.

Before the fire fell, Elijah "stepped forward" in boldness and courage.

This kind of unapologetic individuality was rare in Elijah's day, just like it's rare in ours. While other followers of Yahweh were present on the mountain, and still others who'd not bent a knee to worship Baal were in hiding, running scared from Jezebel's tyranny, Elijah was different. In a time when being clear and unashamed about one's commitment to Yahweh could cost someone his life, Elijah was so committed to his God that the comfort and safety of sameness just wouldn't do. This feature of Elijah's ministry is one of the living, breathing hallmarks that challenges me the most.

Many other memorable personalities in biblical history are also known for stepping forward and standing alone. Choose two of the following passages and use them to do character studies on the people who "stepped forward" and took a lonely stand.

- Numbers 13:26-30
- Esther 4:8-16
- Daniel 6:6-10
- Matthew 14:24-29
- Mark 14:3-9
- Luke 8:43-48

For each one you choose, consider four questions:

1. What did your selected characters do that others didn't, wouldn't, or couldn't?
2. How would hanging back and blending in have been more comfortable and less risky for them? How would it have reduced their exposure?
3. What would likely have been the results of their not stepping forward? What wouldn't have happened, or wouldn't have happened the same way?
4. How did stepping forward cost them? But what did it gain them?

EXAMPLE ONE:

1.

2.

3.

4.

1.

2.

3.

4.

Taken together, what do you learn the most from their examples?

In the margin or another journal, describe how God's Spirit is compelling you to emulate their example in a specific dynamic of your life right now.

Let's take it a step further. Several of the characters in this list (Esther and Daniel, for instance) are remembered for standing boldly and defiantly against hostile government figures, against cultural attacks on the Jewish people. But others of them (like Peter and Caleb) stepped out in bold contrast to the timidity and faithlessness of their own people. This is certainly true of Elijah too. He is not only pictured in stark contrast to the pagan's idolatry but also to Israel's indifference. They had been watching the theatrics of Baal's prophets—Elijah alongside Israel's delegation. Now he stepped forward from *them*. From God's people.

Pay careful attention now. In order to be positioned for the fire Yahweh was sending, Elijah had to distance himself from his fellow countrymen and his fellow followers of Yahweh. At some point one or both of these dynamics will be required of us too.

As the Spirit of God challenges and convicts us toward fearlessness and unashamed commitment, we will frequently need to create distance between ourselves and "our people." Sometimes, in order to be in wholehearted allegiance to our God, we'll have to move away from others with whom we share relationship, whether culturally or spiritually. In this post-Christian era, "stepping forward" will require separation from many who may possess similar beliefs as ours, but who have become apathetic, lukewarm, and watered-down in their commitment to God and His truth.

The kind of boldness that is unashamed of the pure gospel, committed to the inerrancy of God's Word, and unwavering in His standard of holiness will increasingly necessitate a rejection of political correctness and social acceptance. The most stubborn deterrent to receiving the full expression of God's presence and blessing in our lives is the pressure to pursue conformity and acceptance over obedience.

"Post-Christian" culture is one in which a society that once based the majority of its shared ethics and beliefs on a biblical worldview have now marginalized those convictions behind other systems of thought and practice.

How have you recently sensed God leading you to step out in bold faith and belief that will require a clear line of delineation between yourself and "your people"?

"I came to set a man against his father, and a daughter against her mother, and a daughter-in-law against her mother-in-law; and a man's enemies will be the members of his household."

Discuss with your group how you could create the kind of Christian environment where people feel less restrained by the fear and pressure of peers.

MATTHEW 10:35-36

Now let's look again at Elijah's comment in 1 Kings 18:22, printed in the margin. What does this statement tell us about his personal sentiments as he stood on Mount Carmel?

"Elijah said to the people, 'I alone am left a prophet of the LORD, but Baal's prophets are 450 men.'"

1 KINGS 18:22

Given the details in 1 Kings 18:4,20 and 19:18, what was the true reality?

Elijah's wholehearted and unmitigated allegiance was so rare that he felt like he was completely alone, despite the fact that he was surrounded by thousands of others from his own kin and spiritual community. He was the only one standing *here*. He was the only one who "stepped forward" *like this*. He may not have been technically alone, but he sure *felt* like he was. There was no encouragement, no one to stand by him on that mountain. And you'll likely feel the same way, too, whenever you take a bold stance in your faith—on your college campus, in your corporate office, in your artistic field, as part of that organization, or in that family dynamic.

And yet, even as you gear up for the challenge in your own set of unique personal dynamics, remember that there are others—a remnant of us believers who are unashamed and unapologetic. You are not alone even when you feel like you might be. Always remember that your Father has been preparing you for this. The stages of development that we've seen unfolding in Elijah's experience point to it. Every juncture in his life had been designed to cement the boldness of his spiritual backbone so that he'd be fortified to stand in the lone spotlight of Carmel.

> "Turn your loneliness into solitude, and your solitude into prayer."[1]
> —ELISABETH ELLIOT

Think back:

- In *Gilead*, shepherding for lonesome hours on end in the hills and pasturelands

- Under the hot sun at *Cherith*, with only ravens bringing him food

- In *Zarephath*, as an outsider in a foreign land

In each place, Elijah's whole life was instructed and informed by the lessons of solitude. God was his companion and trusted friend when no one else was around to engage in conversation. He learned from hard experience that there was no place he could ever be in the whole wide world and not be in the holy, protective presence of Almighty God.

How have previous seasons of forced or voluntary solitude fortified you for the lifestyle of bold separation that is required of you right now?

Let the powerful words of 2 Chronicles 16:9 foster an eager anticipation in you as you make the hard decisions necessary to step forward with boldness:

> "The eyes of the LORD move to and fro throughout the earth that He may strongly support those whose heart is completely His."
>
> **2 CHRONICLES 16:9**

For Elijah, moments after stepping forward, the "strong support" of Yahweh would fall from an open heaven. And as we step forward, our God will do the same for us.

Pray this:

> *Lord, forgive me for the times when I have chosen the acceptance of my peers over my allegiance to You. Forgive me for melding in seamlessly instead of taking a stand for Your truth. I ask You to empower me by Your Spirit to have a boldness and courage that will not bend in the face of adversity and pressure. My heart is wholly Yours. Show me today what it means to live like it. Give me the spirit of Daniel, Caleb, Esther, and Elijah so that I am unashamed that I am unwilling to be a nominal, lukewarm believer. I want to step forward, out and away from the crowd, and honor You with my whole life. In Jesus' name, amen.*

SIMPLE PRAYER

"Truly I say to you, if you have faith the size of
a mustard seed, you will say to this mountain,
'Move from here to there,' and it will move;
and nothing will be impossible to you."

MATTHEW 17:20b, NASB

A scholarly theologian sat down at his desk to begin working on his newest book. He'd already authored more than a dozen at that point in his career and ministry. His wife walked past the opened office door, casually leaned up against the wall, and asked, "What's this one going to be about?"

"Just Jesus," he responded.

She jokingly ribbed, "Has He changed since the last time you wrote about Him?"

"No," he answered. "But I have."

Our God does not change. Ever. But we most certainly do. He is described as "the Ancient of Days" (Dan. 7:13), meaning that He is everlasting and unchanging. Worthy of our complete trust. We, on the other hand, change as the dynamics of our lives shift from one season to the next. Our needs morph. We grow. Our perspectives broaden. Our interests modify. Our emotions turn. Our ambitions transform. And as a result, the way we relate to God changes. The way we experience and understand Him expands. Not because He has changed, but we have.

Without a doubt, Elijah has been changed leading up to this intense moment on the mountain.

It's already been a long day on Mount Carmel.

It started civilly enough, with an agreement on Elijah's terms of engagement. But then it got rowdy. It got ugly. It got bloody.

Before finally it got quiet. Quiet enough to hear a pagan prophet's pin-sized belief system drop—belief in a lifeless, voiceless, fire-less god that they'd pinned all their prayers on.

Then up stepped Elijah—intentionally, boldly—yet simply and prayerfully.

> "O LORD, the God of Abraham, Isaac and Israel, today let it be known that You are God in Israel and that I am Your servant and I have done all these things at Your word. Answer me, O LORD, answer me, that this people may know that You, O LORD, are God, and that You have turned their heart back again."

1 KINGS 18:36-37

Last week we studied the increasingly raucous pleading that had taken the prophets of Baal all day long to put into words. Today let's look at how the same request took Elijah all of twenty seconds. He spoke it in a prayer that was utterly devoid of high volume or theatrics or worked-up manipulation, like the pagans' prayers had been. It comprised about sixty words, when translated into the English language. His confidence in the ability and authority of Yahweh was so complete that his prayer reverberated with a powerful simplicity, one which stood in stark opposition to those who did not know God.

> Look at the terms used to describe the pleas of Baal's prophets from 1 Kings 18 in the margin. Underline the main descriptive words in each verse.

> Think about the way you tend to relate to God. Does your temperament in prayer generally bear more resemblance to the panic of the prophets of Baal, or to the easy trust of the prophet Elijah?

> How would you say that the confident tone of Elijah's prayer was influenced by what He'd been through in the barrenness of Gilead, the loneliness of Cherith, and the deprivation of Zarephath? What had he learned about God in each place?

"Called on the name of Baal from morning until noon" (v. 26a)

"Leaped about the altar" (v. 26b)

"Cried out with a loud voice and cut themselves" (v. 28)

"Raved until the time of the offering of the evening sacrifice" (v. 29)

Each unique season of Elijah's journey had given the prophet an opportunity to experience Yahweh in a distinctive way—as a provider, a covenant keeper, a protector, and a life-giver. The consistency of his ongoing friendship with his God undergirded this intense moment on Carmel. He didn't need to overcompensate by filling the air with superfluous words. Confident trust had been cemented during these three years. His prayer on Mount Carmel was rooted in relationship, and that's where our prayers can be rooted as well.

Too often we tend to think the only way to get God to move is to pray louder, pray longer, pray harder—to pray as if we're hunting for the right magic words, especially if significant time passes and our wait to see God respond continues. And too often when praying in group settings (as Elijah was doing), our goal is mainly to impress people with our flowery grasp of spiritual vocabulary.

But Elijah's prayer wasn't driven by panic or public approval. Even with the high stakes atop Mount Carmel, he simply rooted his prayer in three important end results. He said, *Lord, answer me so that . . .*

1. YOU WILL BE GLORIFIED.

2. MY RELATIONSHIP WITH YOU WILL BE AFFIRMED.

3. THE PEOPLE'S HEARTS WILL BE TURNED BACK TO YOU.

The most powerful prayers, whether public or private, are the ones devoid of meaningless, pious platitudes. Instead they're simple, assured, and include these three important markers.

1. LORD, ANSWER ME SO THAT . . .

Write down the first goal of prayer on the line provided.

_____

Using the text of Elijah's prayer on the previous page or from your own copy of the Bible (1 Kings 18:36-37), write out the portion (or portions) that underscore the purpose of God being glorified.

If we're honest, sometimes our prayers are watered down with a number of different self-motivated objectives: fulfilling our personal interests, impressing other people, or even just checking a box on our religious to-do list. But Elijah's focus and ultimate goal was spelled out clearly in his simple prayer. His request was unapologetically rooted in a desire for God's authority to be on display and for His magnificence to be amplified before everyone on that mountain.

In other words, the fire itself was not the goal. Elijah wasn't trying to be impressive. The fire was only a means to a greater, more eternal end—for Yahweh to be glorified. What a critical reminder for us!

The ultimate goal of our prayers and requests should mirror Elijah's example. Even as we pray about the most practical aspects of life regarding our children or finances or careers, the ultimate end goal must be to highlight God. To draw attention to *Him*, not us. To magnify *Him*, not us. Reframing our priorities in prayer around this goal will shift much of what we ask Him for and how we approach Him in our asking.

So take inventory of your prayer life today. If you cannot see a clear tie between what you're asking God to do and how He'll be glorified in doing it, you are out of step with the overarching goal of Jesus Himself—namely, "that the Father may be glorified" (John 14:13). If you recognize that you are not in sync with Him in this area, ask His Spirit to adjust the posture of your heart and the priority of your prayers.

Jesus told His disciples to pray like this:

"For thine is the kingdom, and the power, and the glory, for ever. Amen."

MATTHEW 6:13, KJV

> Take a moment to look at each of the following passages. Write down or underline in your Bible the words of each prayer that focus on glorifying the character and faithfulness of God. Use them to format the openings (or closings) of your own personal prayer time today.

• Nehemiah 9:5-8

_____

_____

• Daniel 9:4

_____

_____

Prayer itself is a gift, not an entitlement. It is God's gracious idea for giving us a divinely orchestrated mechanism through which we can have ongoing fellowship with Him and where He allows us to be active participants in the outworking of His purposes on Earth. Prayer is the key that gives us access to experiencing His work in our lives and is always designed to set the stage for Him to be seen more clearly and more fully. This is your Father's goal in prayer. Is it yours?

2. LORD, ANSWER ME SO THAT . . .

Write down the second goal of Elijah's prayer.

_____

Refer back to Elijah's prayer. Write out the portion that speaks to this motive behind his request.

To Ahab, Elijah was the "troubler of Israel" (1 Kings 18:17)—no more than an antagonizing agitator who'd caused unprecedented problems for the nation. But Elijah could weather the sting of such false accusations because he didn't need validation from people in high position. Receiving Yahweh's validation was his chief goal. The highest affirmation he could receive was that of being Yahweh's representative.

So in prayer, after asking God to glorify Himself, Elijah then entreated Him to affirm their relationship. He wanted people to see that his ambitions, endeavors, and pursuits through the years had not been self-motivated or self-created. None of this "troubling," if that's what Ahab insisted on calling it, had been driven by personal agenda or vindication. Elijah had been on a divinely mandated assignment all along. He was God's servant. His ambassador. And now, everyone would know it.

Turn to 2 Corinthians 5:20. What phrase did Paul use to describe himself and his ministry partners?

As Christ's representatives, our prayers should be reflective of our "ambition . . . to be pleasing to Him" (2 Cor. 5:9) and to be validated by Him and Him alone. We are official representatives of our King. And in prayer, our objectives, goals, and interests should always reflect His will.

3. LORD, ANSWER ME SO THAT . . .

Write out Elijah's third objective in prayer.

_____

Last time. Write out the portion of Elijah's prayer that reflects this part of his appeal.

Without a doubt, the prophetic writings of the Old Testament are often filled with hard, challenging statements. Condemnation of sin. Evidence of rebellion. Pronouncements of judgment. Threatening of exile. But read deeper, and you won't hear in God's voice the exasperated disgust of betrayal but the ready solution of repentance.

> "Return to the one the Israelites have greatly rebelled against."
>
> **ISAIAH 31:6, CSB**

> "'Return, faithless people,' declares the LORD, 'for I am your husband.'"
>
> **JEREMIAH 3:14, NIV**

> "Return to the LORD your God, for He is gracious and compassionate, slow to anger, abounding in lovingkindness and relenting of evil."
>
> **JOEL 2:13**

This is God's heart. He wants His people—He wants you and me—responding to Him, _returning_ to Him. Make this simple, heartfelt message a driving motivator behind your prayers: softened hearts, changed minds, and redirected ambitions.

A stunning example of this divine character trait appears just a few chapters later in Elijah's life when God sent him to confront Ahab on a horrific sin—the murder plot against a man who owned a vineyard that Ahab wanted for himself. After Elijah boldly delivered God's word of judgment to the king (_again_)—"This is what the LORD says: 'I am about to bring disaster on you and will eradicate your descendants'" (1 Kings 21:21, CSB)—Ahab's response was completely different than it had been the first time he met the prophet.

"It came about when Ahab heard these words, that he tore his clothes and put on sackcloth and fasted, and he lay in sackcloth and went about despondently. Then the word of the LORD came to Elijah the Tishbite, saying, 'Do you see how Ahab has humbled himself before Me? Because he has humbled himself before Me, I will not bring the evil in his days, but I will bring the evil upon his house in his son's days.'"

1 KINGS 21:27-29

God's desire, even when judgment is warranted, is that people return to Him. No matter who they are or what they've done. We can always know we're praying His heart when we, like Elijah, pray for someone to "turn their heart back again."

The three important elements we've looked at today form a sturdy foundation for simple, powerful, effective praying. As you mature and develop in your relationship with God, let them undergird your conversations with Him.

In closing today, consider two or three of the most pressing requests that you've been making to the Lord recently. What are you praying for?

1.

2.

3.

Now examine your requests in light of the three objectives in Elijah's prayerful example. Over the next few days, for each request, on separate sheets of paper, craft short prayers that align with what you've studied today. Moving forward, use what you've written as a guideline to reframe your prayer life. Confess any way that you've slipped into the panicked, frantic tone of those who do not have confidence in the true and powerful living God. Ask Him to give you wisdom on how to cultivate an effective prayer life that is laced with peace, trust, and the goal of magnifying Him.

THE FIRE FALLS

"Then the fire of the LORD fell and consumed the burnt offering and the wood and the stones and the dust, and licked up the water in the trench."

1 KINGS 18:38

We have a lovely fireplace in our home, which I enjoy nearly every day after the heat of Texas summer has given way to fall and winter. I slip into our living room on most mornings, pull the lever that opens the flue into the chimney, light a long-stemmed match, and touch it to the lowest point of the gas logs. Within moments I'm bathed in warmth and shimmering light. Nice.

But as pretty as it looks and feels, that's about all a fire can do when I'm the one who lights it. Natural fire is limited. It all depends on me. I decide when the time is right for it. And if I can't get it to start for some reason, it's on me to figure out what I'm doing wrong or what needs to be reworked. It's in my hands. I'm responsible for it. And even after I get it going, it only burns temporarily until I make the decision to start it up again, from the bottom—my only access point for lighting it.

This is what distinguishes a man-made fire from God's supernatural fire.

> Look again at 1 Kings 18:23, printed in your margin. What did Elijah tell the people he would deliberately avoid doing to his sacrifice?

"I will prepare the other ox and lay it on the wood, and I will not put a fire under it."

1 KINGS 18:23

Consider Elijah's proactive efforts that we've studied over the past three days. He reverently and intentionally prepared his sacrifice. He stepped out boldly from the silent masses. Then he offered up the simplicity of his believing prayer. But what he did *not* do was come anywhere near that altar bearing the torch of his own fire. He understood that lighting the fire would be to encroach upon margin that belonged to Yahweh alone. His own self-ignited fire would mean nothing. A self-cultivated fire would prove nothing.

God's Spirit enters our soul, stirring in us a holy fervor—first at the moment of our salvation, then more and more as we continue living in alignment with Him and as we continue walking in yielded surrender to Him.

#ElijahBibleStudy

Believer, remember that the fire of God comes *down*, not up. Down from on high. God lights His fire *Himself*—lights it *with* Himself. God's Spirit enters our soul, stirring in us a holy fervor—first at the moment of our salvation, then more and more as we continue living in alignment with Him and as we continue walking in yielded surrender to Him. He graces us with the intangible yet unmistakable mark of His presence on our lives.

The fire that the Spirit ignites burns on. And on. As we experience the undeniable quality of His manifested presence and power increasingly in our lives, we are wooed toward righteousness, not through self-styled legalism but through the organic growth of genuine spiritual fruit, producing in greater abundance every day. God's fire burns out the harmful contaminants that interfere with the purity of our relationship. The only thing our own fire can do is occasionally temper them, these internal enemies that are far too numerous and deeply embedded for us to effectively eliminate. But as the Holy Spirit works, the fire of God's presence and power consumes them all. It wicks them out of our way, leaving Him freedom of movement to infuse us with holy passion for fulfilling our divinely-created purpose.

God's fire is the fire we need. Not *our* fire. *His* fire.

We need the fire to fall.

"The God who answers by fire, He is God."

1 KINGS 18:24

What are some of the ways we try to kindle our own fire as Christians through emotionalism, self-promotion, or religious activity? What does that look like in your own life?

What effects do you think these ongoing, unsuccessful efforts make on us as believers, in terms of our emotional stability, our spiritual encouragement, our contentment and peace?

Fire is often directly and indirectly tied to the might and ministry of the Holy Spirit working in the life of a believer. In the Book of Acts, Jesus gathered the disciples together and commanded them not to leave Jerusalem until they'd received what the Father had promised them: "You will receive power when the Holy Spirit has come upon you" (Acts 1:8). Then on the Day of Pentecost, the Holy Spirit appeared to them "like flames of fire that separated and rested on each one of them" (Acts 2:3, CSB).

But this symbolism did not begin in the first century AD. Long before, throughout the Old Testament, fire was already symbolic of God's authentic power and His manifest presence. It was the sign of Yahweh's habitation with humanity—His approval, His favor, His nearness.

> Look up each of these brief references from scriptural events that occurred long before Elijah's episode on Mount Carmel. You don't need to stay in any one place long. Just jot beside each reference key words that are significant about the appearance of the fire.
>
> • Exodus 3:1-4
>
> • Exodus 13:20-22
>
> • Exodus 19:18-19
>
> • Leviticus 9:23-24
>
> • 2 Chronicles 7:1-3
>
> Now think about what God accomplished on each occasion. To the left side of each reference above, write the letter that corresponds. There may be more than one answer that applies to each.
>
> A. God's redirection   D. God's consuming power
> B. God's leading   E. God's glory and power
> C. God's voice

Every Israelite in attendance on Mount Carmel that day with Elijah would've known about these holy encounters you just studied.

So when he announced what the grand finale of the day's event would be—"the God who answers by fire, He is God"—they would've warmed with holy anticipation at the possibility of seeing this divine occurrence with their own eyes. To them, it signified the full expression of God's presence with them.

And then it happened:

> "The fire of the LORD fell and consumed the burnt offering and the wood and the stones and the dust, and licked up the water that was in the trench."

1 KINGS 18:38

In the verse above, underline the elements that God's holy fire consumed.

It completely consumed the expected things. But it also consumed things that don't usually burn. Solid rock, for example—those twelve stones that corresponded to the twelve tribes of Israel, reinforcing the promise-keeping power of His unbreakable covenant. The fire of God also "licked up" the water. And suddenly, in an instant, those thirsty Israelites—who'd come here thinking only of quenching their thirst after 1,277 days without rain—weren't thinking about that at all anymore.

> "When all the people saw it, they fell facedown and said, 'The LORD, he is God! The LORD, he is God!'"

1 KINGS 18:39

Because that's what the fire of God does. It draws glorious attention to Him and Him alone.

That's why I want it. That's why we need it. That's why He sends it—so that regular humans like you and me can become living, breathing billboards of His manifest presence, and so that we can know what it's like to walk in divine power in everything we do. As we go throughout the rhythm of our daily lives with the presence of God's Spirit oozing out of us—His fruit, His gifts, His goodness, His power—the people in our sphere of influence will see the witness of His Spirit upon us and be compelled to declare, "The LORD, he is God! The LORD, he is God!" Mere talent, hard work, or busyness cannot produce this type of responsive effect.

As I write this lesson to you, I am startlingly aware of this holy reality in my own life and ministry. As my mind is frantically attempting to digest and clearly deliver all the content I've studied and the biblical insight I've tried to glean, I realize my best attempt at this work will be fruitless if God's Spirit doesn't rest His hand upon it. We will both have wasted our time—a series of weeks for you, and a couple of consecutive years for me—if the fire doesn't fall, if the blessing of God does not anoint these devotionals so that their messages are seared within your heart by the Holy Spirit Himself. And so I've recognized (and confessed to Him) my tendency to overwork and under-pray. To overproduce and under-consecrate.

But more and more, I'm learning that holiness and godly priorities will produce what all my extra hours of work never could. That's what I dearly, desperately want. I want the unmistakable mark of God's presence to rest here with me, not only when I'm writing or teaching, but when I'm being a mother and wife, sister and friend—in other words, all the time, in all the regular rhythms of daily life.

I know you want this too. And our Father offers this experience through His manifest presence with us. Daily. Moment by moment. So let's look to Elijah's example, doing our part as we trust God to do His.

1. PRESENT YOUR FULL SELF TO GOD—your time, talents and treasures—as a living sacrifice. Not haphazardly, but intentionally and thoughtfully.

2. BE UNASHAMED—public and bold in your allegiance to Him.

3. COMMIT TO THE SPIRITUAL DISCIPLINES that cultivate an ongoing, vibrant relationship with God: prayer, Bible reading, humility, and surrender.

Sister, there is grace for these lifestyle choices and patterns. He Himself will walk alongside you as you choose this framework for your life. So don't feel burdened by a spiritual to-do list. Instead relax and enjoy your friendship with God in these consistent ways.

He is *for* you, and His fire is already falling down upon you.

KEEP THE FIRE GOING

"Do not let one of them escape."

1 KINGS 18:40b

The previous owners of our current home left behind an outdoor firepit. I was so glad to see that it was still in the backyard when we moved in. Every so often when we have the time, we'll sit around it on the back patio with metal sticks in hand, roasting marshmallows for s'mores.

I'll never forget the first time we tried to use it. We were so excited. Fire, outdoors, under a blanketing sky—like the country in the city. But no matter what my husband did to kindle that dim flicker of light into a roaring fire that night, nothing worked. He tried several different tricks of his, even resorting to using some starter squares, but still no fire.

That's when we figured out the problem. *The wood was damp.* A thunderstorm the previous night had dropped a good dousing on our uncovered stack of firewood. We knew that. But it hadn't seemed damp to the touch. After seventeen hours of drying out, we figured it would be more than able to burn by now. But it wasn't. The only way we were going to keep and cultivate any fire in the firepit that night was to get rid of the wet wood that was working against it.

Entirely. Log by log.

All of it.

I thought of that evening as I was studying the closing scene of Elijah's confrontation with the prophets of Baal. The glorious fire had come down on Mount Carmel, and the crowd had been awestruck with wonder. Israel's people fell to the ground in worship, while the prophets of Baal stood by.

The spiritual fire had been ignited, but Elijah's assignment was not yet complete. These holy flames of revival needed the right atmosphere in order to keep burning. Anything and everything working against it needed to be removed.

Completely.

> Elijah said to them, "Seize the prophets of Baal; do not let one of them escape." So they seized them; and Elijah brought them down to the brook Kishon, and slew them there.
>
> **1 KINGS 18:40**

Sound extreme? Yes. But this severe effort was a required element of Elijah's assignment. And it will be ours if we want to cultivate the fire. We must annihilate anything and everything that keeps the fire of God's Spirit from burning brightly and continuously in our lives.

> Before you move forward into today's devotional, consider any habit, attitude, unmanaged desire, or illegitimate relationship that you've allowed to "escape" and go unattended. What are these things that dull your spiritual passion and zeal? Below and continuing into the margin, begin an honest list of the things in your life that (1) do not foster God's fire in you or (2) actively contribute to its diminished fervor.

Picture the sight of these thousands of Israelites in the foreground, falling on their faces and declaring, "The LORD, he is God! The LORD, he is God!" (v. 39), while those hundreds of prophets of Baal stood erect, in shock, unyielding in the background. The stark contrast made their irreverence clear. They still refused to abandon their mission. And Elijah knew if they escaped—even one of them—they would continue to be what F. B. Meyer called "agents of apostasy."[2] It would only be a matter of time before idol worship threaded its way back into the full tapestry of Israel's fabric. He could not let that happen.

And neither can we.

It's difficult to reconcile the grace and goodness of Yahweh with His command to annihilate an entire people group. But remember, He had delayed justice for their rebellion, giving them opportunity for repentance before deeming their cup of iniquity full (see Gen. 15:16; Jonah 3:4), before releasing a divine judgment.

It can be hard to absorb the need for such a gruesome and horrific assassination. Mass slaying. And yet removing the poison, removing it *entirely*, was necessary if the people were to move forward in a healthy spiritual direction.

Let's take a look at how this precedent ran throughout all of Israel's history and why it was so critical in cementing their loyalty to Yahweh.

Turn to 1 Samuel 15 and read the following verses, answering the accompanying questions:

Verses 1-4: What did God command His people to do?

Verse 9: How did they respond?

Now flip over to 1 Samuel 30:1-3. What effect did the Amalekites have on Israel in the future?

Another episode that pinpoints a similar grievance is seen in the Israelites' relationship with the Midianites. Their history with one another revealed a time of distant friendship between these two people groups. Moses, for example, invited his father-in-law, who was a Midianite priest-prince, to join Israel in her venture to the promised land. Many other Midianites also accepted this invitation. There are even indications that the Lord's acts during the wilderness journey began to sway these pagan people toward a belief in Yahweh (see Ex. 18:10-12). But this influence was soon stunted, and the Midianites became one of the primary corrupters of Israel.

Why the history lesson? Because of how it helps us interpret the Hebrews' response to God's instructions concerning Midian near the end of Moses' life, and possibly why the Israelites' troubles had persisted into future generations. Let's take a look.

What were God's instructions to Moses in Numbers 31:1-5?

What did Israel do in response to this command (vv. 7-15)?

○ Slaughtered all the males
○ Spared the women and children
○ Killed the kings
○ Plundered the city and took the bounty for themselves

Of the options you chose, which one did Moses call out in verse 15 as a violation of God's command, as a problem?

How might Israel's initial relationship with Midian have played a part in Israel's not following through completely with God's instructions?

In each case, both with the Amalekites and the Midianites, the divine mandate to completely destroy them was only partially carried out. In the case of Midian, even though Moses sought to rectify the people's decisions after the fact, it's possible the small remnant left behind, along with the nomadic Midianite population, was enough to reinvent this fierce tribe of people who would seek vengeance on Israel during the time when the judges ruled. By the time those days rolled around, the Midianites had become "as numerous as the sand on the seashore" (Judg. 7:12), terrorizing God's people.

Do you see? Israel's penchant for leaving God's business half-done created a ripple effect of consequences that lasted for generations. Because of the idolatrous influences of their neighbors, Israel found it increasingly difficult to commit to the unhindered worship of Yahweh. Before long, they'd almost completely slipped into Baal worship, walking deeper and deeper into the religious lifestyle patterns of their new neighbors. In addition, they were constantly threatened militarily by the surrounding armies. Between the moral decay and the ongoing military danger, God's chosen were compromised, both spiritually and physically.

The Midianites would later attack and pillage the Israelites for seven consecutive years (Judg. 6:1 and following), wreaking havoc on their nation and families. Yahweh would raise up a deliverer named Gideon to bring victory back to the nation of Israel.

From the previous paragraph, list two of the effects of Israel's disobedience.

1.

2.

Earlier today, you wrote down certain areas that you've let slip under the radar and remain unaddressed, untamed, as you seek to maintain holy fire in your life. Consider them now in light of the two observations you just noted. How has your slowness or unwillingness to deal decisively with these things had a similar weakening effect on you?

1.

2.

God can see into the future, you know. He can already tell you about the negative effects these loose ends will create. So we must trust His intel fully—completely enough to get rid of *any* habit, affiliation, attitude, or life direction that is simply too toxic and needs to be obliterated from our lives. Not in bits and pieces (even though complete emotional separation may take time and continued accountability) but in total. To the fullest extent. Despite how harsh, excessive, drastic, or merely unnecessary this total severing may appear, honoring Him by your obedience will save you from future issues you cannot (but He can) foresee.

Today would be a good day to take some things down to your own brook of Kishon, and to come back empty-handed. To come back free. For good.

For the past two weeks of our Bible study, we've stood on Mount Carmel and we've seen fire rain down from heaven. I'm praying our time here has stirred a fervor in your heart, just like it's done in mine. From this point forward, as we continue to yield to the work of the Holy Spirit, our assignment is to cooperate with Him—"to fan into flame the gift of God" (2 Tim. 1:6, ESV)—by cultivating that relationship through His Word and prayer, and by proactively severing our own "prophets of Baal" who, left unchecked, will dampen the flame.

Culminate your week of Bible study by prayerfully reading through the following passage from Paul in Galatians 5, seeing how the tendencies of the flesh actively work against the work of the Spirit.

"For the flesh sets its desire against the Spirit, and the Spirit against the flesh; for these are in opposition to one another, so that you may not do the things that you please. But if you are led by the Spirit, you are not under the Law. Now the deeds of the flesh are evident, which are: immorality, impurity, sensuality, idolatry, sorcery, enmities, strife, jealousy, outbursts of anger, disputes, dissensions, factions, envying, drunkenness, carousing, and things like these, of which I forewarn you, just as I have forewarned you, that those who practice such things will not inherit the kingdom of God."

GALATIANS 5:17-21

Now in the words of Elijah, refuse to "let one of them escape." Circle any actions of the flesh listed in the Galatians passage that the Holy Spirit is asking you to seize and slaughter.

Who are some people in your circle of influence that you can enlist to help hold you accountable in these areas?

As you begin to think proactively about how you can follow through, don't slip into worry or a sense of being overwhelmed. Rest and trust. God's Spirit lives in you. He sent the fire, and He will keep it tended. He will give you clarity on how to honor His instructions, as well as the courage to keep going. Then as you commit to the progressive, systematic annihilation of these idols, you will open up the way for God's blessings in your experience.

Just ask godly Elijah. Or you can even ask godless Ahab.

Either one of them could tell you . . .

RAIN IS COMING.

THE HOLY SPIRIT AND FIRE

Throughout the Old Testament, fire symbolized the manifest presence of the Lord among humanity, not only with Elijah on Mount Carmel but in varying locations and time periods.

Take, for example, God's appearance to Moses from within a burning bush in the desert of Horeb (Ex. 3:2), the fire that fell while Moses and his brother Aaron were serving in the tabernacle (Lev. 9:23), and the fire that consumed the sacrifices on the altar when Solomon dedicated the temple (2 Chron. 7:1). In each case, and many others, fire was the tangible representation of Yahweh's nearness and a sign of His approval and acceptance. His presence rendered the soil holy, and everyone in the vicinity was compelled to fall to the ground in reverence. Flesh trembled as Yahweh's holy fire purified, refined, directed, and consumed. These flames could not be crafted by the skillful hands of craftsmen, nor could they be conjured up through the impressive wisdom of kings. The fire was a divine gift, initiated and offered by God alone.

This symbolism continued into the New Testament, where fire is often tied to the ministry of the Holy Spirit in the life of a believer, beginning on the Day of Pentecost (Acts 2). As one scholar summarized, "The zeal of service, the flame of love, the fervour of prayer, the earnestness of testimony, the devotion of consecration, the sacrifice of worship, and the igniting-power of influence are attributable to the Spirit."[3]

To be clear, the Holy Spirit was given to you and me as a gift of our salvation:

"In Him, you also, after listening to the message of truth, the gospel of your salvation—having also believed, you were sealed in Him with the Holy Spirit of promise, who is given as a pledge of our inheritance, with a view to the redemption of God's own possession, to the praise of His glory."
EPHESIANS 1:13-14

As Christ followers, the Holy Spirit is in us. *All* of Him. But He is only reflected *upon and through* us to the extent that we allow Him to be. By this I mean that only those who choose a lifestyle of yielded obedience have the opportunity to walk in the full expression of His work in their lives.

We know from Scripture, for instance, that we can "grieve" the Holy Spirit (Eph. 4:30-32), and that we can "quench" the fire of the Spirit from burning brightly in us (1 Thess. 5:19). But as we continue to yield to Him—by heeding His conviction, relying on Him for daily empowerment, and cultivating a fervent friendship—we are "filled with the Spirit" (Eph. 5:18) until His presence overflows in our actions, attitudes, and ambitions. His fruit and His gifts become outworked through our lives. We are graced with His visible favor and empowerment. Our efforts are no longer fueled by mere talent and sweat equity, but they become marked by a divine approval that reverberates with the Father's applause. This is how our whole lives become infused and saturated with purpose, glorifying to the Father, and able to bear eternal fruit. As we follow Elijah's example of humility and integrity, and as we intentionally present a "living sacrifice" of our whole selves to God (Rom. 12:1), we invite the fire of God's presence to consume us.

With our achievement-oriented culture of perfectly-lit selfies and staged personas, it can be easy to assume a veneer of religion and pseudo-sacred activity that appears to spew smoke signals of authentic holy flames. But we must resist the urge to mask any lack of authentic intimacy with God by fabricating our own false flames through emotionalism and self-promotion. *His* fire is what we need if we expect to live up to our calling and experience the freedom of serving others with selfless joy and *real* power. Yes, we must do our part diligently (prepare the sacrifice), but then we leave room for the Father to do His (ignite the fire).

Time and eternity will draw a clear distinction between what He has done and what we have manufactured on our own. If the fire is not authentic—if it is by our "might" and our "power" but not by His "Spirit" (Zech. 4:6)—it will eventually flicker and fail.

Horeb

FEAR, FATIGUE, AND A FUTURE

WEEK SIX

DO YOU HEAR WHAT I HEAR?

1. God said it; let's _____ it (1 Kings 18:41).

*You don't adapt to your _____. As you live in light of
God's _____, your surroundings need to begin to adapt to you,
as you communicate God's _____ and His promises clearly.*

*It requires spiritual _____. It requires _____ _____,
to be able to see the things that cannot be seen in the physical realm, to be
able to hear the things you cannot hear unless the Holy Spirit heightened
your spiritual ears.*

**2. God said it; let's _____ in _____ with it
    (1 Kings 18:42).**

*His promises are what ignite our prayer lives with an extra measure of
_____ and _____ as we pray.*

Base your prayers directly on the _____ of God.

3. God said it; let's _____ for it (1 Kings 18:43).

*Be always _____ of how what's happening could be _____ to
what you've _____.*

4. God said it; let's _____ _____ for it (1 Kings 18:44).

*Faith is acting like it _____ _____, even when it's _____
_____, so that it might _____ _____, simply
because God _____ _____.*

Video and audio sessions available for purchase
and rent at LifeWay.com/Elijah.

REST AWHILE

"Come with me by yourselves to
a quiet place and get some rest."

MARK 6:31, NIV

I spent the summer of 2015 filming a movie called *War Room*. I was a rookie as an actress and enjoyed every minute of the unique challenge laid out before me each thirteen-hour day. The cast and crew started in the early morning (except for the scenes we had to shoot all night!) with a devotional over a light breakfast, before launching into the triple-digit heat to get our work done. For ten solid weeks, all hands were on deck to accomplish a common goal: producing a film that would glorify God in the most excellent way possible.

And then, one day at the close of July, we were finished. *That's a wrap.* We said sorrowful goodbyes to one another and headed back to our respective cities.

But I'll never forget the morning after I got home. I woke up feeling nearly the same way as I felt after delivering my babies—as if I'd been hit by a truck. My muscles were sore, my eyes were red, the lids slightly swollen. I was dehydrated, which made my digestive system sluggish and resistant to doing its job. I also nursed an ongoing slight headache, and my joints felt tight and achy. For weeks actually, I had trouble making it through the day without a short afternoon nap. Even my mind seemed too numb to process anything other than the latest episode of *Fixer Upper*. I was toast. Soggy toast.

Tired.

As this recovery period lingered on, much longer than I'd expected, I was about to start feeling guilt over my lack of productivity. But then I remembered what the film's wise producer had told me, *before* filming had ever begun, knowing I'd need the caution later. "You're human," he'd said. "*Prepare* to give yourself a break."

ELIJAH

I'm wondering if this week of study intersects with your life during a season of exhaustion. Maybe you've extended yourself relationally, creatively, or financially, in ways that have left you feeling depleted, even decimated. If that's *you* today, I just want to tell you to curl up safely and soundly in your Father's grace, and hear Him whisper to you . . .

REST.

In one of their most intimate exchanges, this is exactly what Yahweh encouraged for Elijah.

> As we move into 1 Kings 19, identify the following happenings in Elijah's life from the end of the previous chapter. Start in 1 Kings 18:40.
>
> • Verse 40: He _____ the prophets of _____.
> • Verse 41: He met again with _____.
> • Verse 42: He climbed to the top of _____ and he
>   _____.
> • Verse 43: He sent his servant to look for rain clouds
>   _____ times.
> • Verse 44: He dispatched a follow-up message to
>   _____.
> • Verse 45: He watched the sky grow _____ with
>   clouds and wind.
> • Verse 46: He _____ all the way to _____.

While Elijah engaged in all this activity, he told Ahab to refresh himself with food and drink (1 Kings 18:41-42) while Elijah returned to the summit of Carmel to pray fervently for rain. Between the spiritual battle he'd just been through on Mount Carmel and the physical energy he'd expended in running eighteen miles to Jezreel, the Bible says nothing about Elijah stopping to sleep, eat, or get a drink of water. He simply kept going.

> Take a moment to go to your map on the inside back cover and find the location of Jezreel to track Elijah's movements.

Elijah had suggested that someone else (Ahab) take time to eat and drink, and yet Elijah hadn't taken his own advice. In what ways do you tend to take care of the basic needs of others while ignoring your own?

Turn to Mark 6, a chapter which chronicles an exceptionally busy season of ministry for Jesus' twelve disciples. Read verses 7-13, as well as verses 30-31, then come back here to answer the following questions:

- What had the disciples been busy doing?

- What had they neglected to do?

- What advice did Jesus give them?

Like the disciples, you'll undoubtedly encounter seasons of life that require more of you than other times, when you need to push yourself past where you think your body can go. But don't convince yourself that by virtue of being a Christian, you are immune from needing to consider your physical needs. Burnout is not a sign of spirituality. That is a fallacy, and it is dangerous. Sooner or later, the neglect will catch up to you.

> "For he knows our frame; he remembers that we are dust."
>
> PSALM 103:14, ESV

God knows that we are human. His Spirit lives in us, yes, but we can only be as effective as our physical bodies will allow. We so often look for some hidden, spiritual reason to explain our weariness and our touch-iness and our increased susceptibility to selfish attitudes and behavior, rather than consider it's likely the result of neglecting obvious physical needs. This natural reality explains, at least in part, why a rock-solid, fire-hardened Elijah would run in fear for his life from the mere sound of Jezebel's message. He was flat-out tired. And hungry.

It's not unspiritual to tend to our physical, emotional, and mental frame. And in one of my favorite portions of Elijah's narrative, Yahweh's response to the prophet is about to show us that. First, however, let's learn from a couple of counterproductive things Elijah did that enhanced his compromised condition.

1. ALL BY MYSELF

"When he came to Beersheba that belonged to Judah, he left his servant there."

1 KINGS 19:3b

Look at your map again and find Beersheba. Draw a jagged line from Jezreel to this location.

What did Elijah do when he got there?

When discouragement sets in, most people tend toward one of two relational extremes. They either (1) pad their despair with unhealthy or excessive amounts of people, or (2) become an island, peeling off by themselves and isolating further. Elijah, feeling as though he'd been abandoned by everyone anyway, chose to separate from his sole companion.

Which is your usual go-to option? Fight discouragement by adding more people, or soothe yourself with more isolation?

Make a list of pros and cons regarding whichever tendency you hover toward.

HOW DOES IT SERVE YOU?	HOW DOES IT HURT YOU?

One of the enemy's driving motivations is to bring division within the body of Christ—to isolate whole groups of us from others for illegitimate reasons, or to create fissures in healthy interpersonal relationships where caring support would otherwise occur. Unity among brothers and sisters in Christ forms a firm line of defense against Satan's advances, and he knows it. That's why he bristles against it.

So when you're in a place in life where you're feeling completely worn out, one of his leading lies will encourage you to overinflate your belief that there's no one else who can understand what you're facing. *No one. You're on your own now, buddy.* That's exactly where we find Elijah in 1 Kings 19. His despair had distorted his perspective enough until he felt he was "the only one left" (v. 14, NIV) who was devoted to God.

"Two are better than one because they have a good return for their labor. For if either of them falls, the one will lift up his companion. But woe to the one who falls when there is not another to lift him up. Furthermore, if two lie down together they keep warm, but how can one be warm alone? And if one can overpower him who is alone, two can resist him. A cord of three strands is not quickly torn apart."

ECCLESIASTES 4:9-12

According to 1 Kings 19:18, what was the truth?

Read forward to verses 19-21. What did he gain that further discredited his self-pitying perspective?

How do you find this same distorted perspective taking shape in your own thinking when you're discouraged, tired, or overwhelmed?

Read the passage from Ecclesiastes 4 in the margin. Write down any observations you make from it. Prayerfully consider if a fractured friendship or relationship in your life reveals the enemy's handiwork in separating you from needed reinforcement (and separating them from yours).

Write down something practical you can do *today* to counteract the enemy's goal and retain this relationship (if possible)?

If you're participating in this study with a group, the women around you are partners in this season of your journey. They are part of what God has given you to offer encouragement, strength, realignment, restoration, and so much more. While adding unhealthy or unnecessary relationships to your life is not beneficial during difficult seasons of life, neither is pushing away godly friendships that hold you accountable and help facilitate emotional stability. Learn a hard, raw lesson from Elijah: *Don't isolate.*

2. MISPLACED EXPECTATIONS

Elijah had honored Yahweh's instructions to the best of his ability at every step of the way. And yet he appears to have done so with unspoken, maybe even subconscious expectations about what the end results would be.

He'd understandably hoped that his actions would precipitate an immediate national revival, the kind where people in every crevice of the Israelite community, from the top rungs of government on down, would pledge their complete allegiance to the one true God. Initially that's what the people had *said* on Mount Carmel.

But the king had feasted and not repented, and Jezebel was still on her rampage. Things just hadn't panned out the way Elijah expected. And the disappointment was killing him.

Focus in on Elijah's final comment in verse 4. What comparison was he making?

"He went on a day's journey into the wilderness. He sat down under a broom tree and prayed that he might die. He said, 'I have had enough! LORD, take my life, for I am no better than my fathers.'"

1 KINGS 19:4, CSB

In each of the following areas, consider any preset expectations you may have inadvertently imposed on God or yourself.

- The outcome of your ministry
- The life of your children
- The trajectory of your career
- The future of your marriage

Is there any way that comparison with others—whether they are peers or from a previous generation—has contributed to your dashed expectations?

For Elijah, this season of fatigue uncovered an inflated ego underneath his tough exterior. Apparently some of his devastation extended from not doing better than his forefathers—from not quickly and completely leading Israel back to God. He thought his ministry would be different. Better than theirs. The first of its kind. But comparison and misplaced expectations had derailed his emotional stability. He was pummeled with self-condemnation, disappointment, and regret about his failure to achieve something that God never even expected of him.

And now, in this critical moment of the prophet's life—when he was the most depleted, vulnerable, fatigued, depressed, and disillusioned—Yahweh stepped in with practical nourishment. He didn't rebuke him, nor did he ignore or discard him. Instead, watch with me as He refreshes him with the most basic of human needs.

After reading 1 Kings 19:5-9, spend your last few minutes of time today with these questions:

What did God allow Elijah to do?

What did He make provision for Elijah to have?

What does this reveal about how Yahweh viewed His prophet's depleted state?

How does Yahweh's response to Elijah in the Old Testament mirror Jesus' response to the disciples in the New Testament?

How does His reaction to Elijah give you a sense of freedom regarding your own limitations and humanity?

With as many profound principles as we've gleaned from Elijah's narrative over the past six weeks, I wouldn't be surprised if this one is the most liberating you've experienced thus far. God is not mad at you because your body is tired or your mind is frayed or your soul is unusually heavy—not after the kind of project you've just finished, or the difficulties you've just endured, or the emotional marathon you've just run. He isn't agitated by the limitations of your flesh. Instead, He stands patiently ready to minister to you, to work through those deficiencies, and to nourish you as you recover from them.

With all the busyness, legalism, strictness, and tension that may be an ongoing part of your daily life, take a moment to breathe deeply, enjoying the gracious and sincere affection of your Father today. He sees. He knows.

> "He restores my soul."
>
> **PSALM 23:3**

Sister, rest.

And while you're at it, "Eat, because the journey is too great for you" (v. 7).

Nothing unspiritual about that.

OFF MESSAGE

"Jezebel sent a messenger to Elijah."

1 KINGS 19:2

Ever felt an adrenaline rush? I'm sure you have—that sudden, biochemical surge of hormones into your bloodstream that naturally occurs during intense moments of stress, fear, challenge, or excitement. Your heart races. Your breath quickens. Your hands may even shake. But although the physical sensation itself can be unsettling and nerve-wracking, an adrenaline rush is actually a good thing. It boosts your energy for completing overwhelming tasks, while muting your body's ability to feel pain or exhaustion. It's our Creator's way of helping increase our strength and performance capabilities so we can accomplish things we didn't know we could do or make it through.

But the *backside* of this rush can be difficult to handle too. Ask me how I know.

Whenever I finish an event or project that's required a large investment of emotional or physical energy, fueled by adrenaline for hours at a time, all I usually feel like doing in the letdown period that follows is feeding my flesh. Give me sleep. Give me food. Give me television. Give me space.

There's nothing wrong with resting, of course. We need that. Resting replenishes. Resting builds us back up. But if we're not on guard, we'll overreact to the rush of adrenaline we feel as our circumstances begin normalizing into the rhythm of a daily routine. We'll crash. We'll spiral into an emotional tailspin, becoming obsessively self-critical and hyper-sensitive, crippled by insecurity, giving into overindulgence, loneliness, and even paralyzing sadness.

Vulnerable.

Really, this vulnerability is what can become a gateway for further issues. The letdown from an adrenaline rush can crack open a door that gives the enemy unique access to our heart and mind, to the driver's seat of our soul.

Fair to say, this is what happened to Elijah, at least in part, after all he'd endured on Mount Carmel.

Before we dive back into Elijah's narrative, take a few moments for some self-inventory.

- What are the greatest struggles you typically face during the aftermath of an adrenaline rush? What unruly desires are you most susceptible to satisfy? After you write them all down, circle the one that is most severe.

- How does the enemy seek to take advantage of your vulnerability by feeding you untrue suggestions or attractive temptations?

- What thought patterns and/or destructive behaviors become harder to ignore or overcome than at other times?

Now let's get back to Elijah. His journey up to this point has been punctuated by one extreme scenario after another. When you take into account the cumulative effects of what he'd faced during his ministry, he had truly been operating on bionic-level doses of adrenaline for several years. It's understandable, then, that the next chapter would begin to chronicle his crash. And in a way, I'm grateful that it does. Because it reminds us that *everyone*—even mighty representatives of God who are on mission and fulfilling their divine assignments—are still human and in need of safeguarding.

> Even mighty representatives of God who are on mission and fulfilling their divine assignments are still human and in need of safeguarding.

But today I want you to see how Elijah's natural vulnerability intersected with something—with *someone*—that pushed him over the edge.

Read 1 Kings 19:1-3. What does this passage indicate as the tipping point that brought on Elijah's meltdown?

> "And he was afraid and arose and ran for his life and came to Beersheba, which belongs to Judah, and left his servant there."
>
> 1 KINGS 19:3

Underline the descriptive phrases from verse 3 that reveal his emotional response and the actions it led to. Below, add any depth about what Elijah's actions reveal.

In only a few short verses, the same man who "outran Ahab" into town after the arrival of a rainstorm (1 Kings 18:46) has turned into a man who "ran for his life." Despite the Lord's hand still being on him—which it is—there's certainly a marked difference in this version of God's prophet. The bold, fearless, prayer-warrior prophet of God has become fragile, insecure, and depressed. The question is: *Why?*

Answer: Because in this moment of understandable exhaustion and emotional depletion, his primary enemy sent him a message. And not only did the message get through to him, but . . .

He believed it.

Read 1 Kings 19:2 again. Write out Jezebel's threat to Elijah word-for-word in the space below.

Take a look at 2 Kings 2:10-11, which chronicles Elijah's last moments on Earth. What light does this shed on the veracity of Jezebel's threat?

Brace yourself against the enemy's message.

Jezebel's contempt for Elijah had been boiling for a long time. She already despised him for his bold stance on the side of Yahweh during three contentious, continuous years without rain. She was even more furious now at how he'd embarrassed her beloved prophets of Baal in the showdown on Mount Carmel—the same prophets she'd invested her time and personal finances to support. And when her weak, spineless husband came whining to her about how Elijah had seized and slaughtered those same defeated prophets in the Kishon Valley, her fury soared off the charts.

ELIJAH

Elijah was going to pay. Elijah must suffer.

Please notice that she didn't send a hit man. She didn't rally a squadron of mercenaries to surround him. She *could* have done those things, because she obviously knew his location. But it's clear that she wasn't as interested in delivering the edge of a sword as she was in delivering a carefully worded message. Instead of going to the trouble of killing him, she knew that the *threat* of death would be a worse punishment than death itself. She didn't need to kill Elijah if she could demoralize, discourage, and derail him enough to want to kill himself. And as much as I hate to say it, she was right.

What did Elijah pray for in 1 Kings 19:4?

Jezebel's tactics are actually an Old Testament example of a New Testament principle and warning—a demonic ploy still used against the people of God to this day. The devil is our enemy, our "adversary." He is hoping that the lies he suggests and the methods of discouragement he employs will lead God's people to despondency and hopelessness.

As Christians, we cannot be destroyed. Our eternal destiny is secured. But if we are not on guard, proactively rehearsing and renewing our minds with God's promises, the enemy's threats will take root and blossom into full-blown despair. Especially in seasons of vulnerability.

Such was the case with Elijah. Despite the victory and fortitude he exhibited on Carmel, his fragility proved a perfect breeding ground for Jezebel's lie. With the door opened after his adrenaline crash, her message had all the nutrients it needed in order to take root, fester, and mushroom out of control. This way, he'd turn into a fear-ridden fugitive running away into the wilderness. He'd be robbed of the confidence, peace, and vision for remaining effective as a prophet. He'd be eaten up with too much anxiety and apprehension to get back in the fray again.

If her message could make him afraid enough, he'd forget what God had already done. In Cherith. In Zarephath. On Carmel. And the prophet would stop trusting Him with the future.

> "Your adversary, the devil, prowls around like a roaring lion, seeking someone to devour."
>
> **1 PETER 5:8**

The devil is constantly "prowling," assuming a posture that is menacing and threatening. He is hunting with intention to kill—"seeking" to devour, though not actually doing it.

Earlier in today's lesson, you circled the biggest struggle you face when you are vulnerable emotionally, mentally, or physically. Write it in the margin here. Now choose two or three of the following passages to look up, write down, and rehearse regularly, in order to keep yourself fortified and on a path of victory and freedom even when spiritually threatened.

- Exodus 14:13-14,23-25
- Psalm 118:1-7
- Romans 8:31-39
- Ephesians 6:10-13
- Philippians 4:19
- Hebrews 12:1-3

During the times when you are weakened, whether physically or emotionally, you must be intentional about girding yourself against the enemy's schemes. Put on the full armor of God and be vigilant about it. Make sure that you are fitted securely with the helmet of salvation so that your mind remains protected against his lies and attempts to take advantage of you. When you sense thoughts and ideas bombarding your mind that are contrary to how the Bible defines your identity in Christ and His nature toward you—especially after a season of success OR a period of extreme difficulty and hardship—prepare in advance to immediately discard the devil's deceptions. He is hoping you'll let down your guard in times of exhaustion so that you'll believe his lies and threats over the truths of God.

Remember this:

"The weapons of our warfare are not of the flesh, but divinely powerful for the destruction of fortresses. We are destroying speculations and every lofty thing raised up against the knowledge of God, and we are taking every thought captive to the obedience of Christ."

2 CORINTHIANS 10:4-5

You don't have to cave to his threats. You can be strong, even when you're weak. Fortify yourself in specific, strategic prayer. Arm yourself with specific promises from God's Word, asking His Spirit to guide you to places in His Word that directly refute the enemy's messaging. Consistently rehearse what God has already done on your behalf.

Defeat the message, and you'll defeat the messenger.

LOCATION SERVICES

"Then he came there to a cave and lodged there;
and behold, the word of the Lord came to him."

1 KINGS 19:9

One of the most meaningful aspects of our redemption in Christ is that you and I can never reach a place so far away that we're beyond the reach of our Father's love, grace, and mercy. This gospel truth brings tears to my eyes when I contemplate the fact that He can reach me wherever I am, no matter how bleak or dry the wilderness I'm traveling through.

David captured it well when he said,

> "Where can I go from Your Spirit? Or where can I flee from Your presence? If I ascend to heaven, You are there; If I make my bed in Sheol, behold, You are there. . . . If I say, 'Surely the darkness will overwhelm me, and the light around me will be night,' even the darkness is not dark to You, and the night is as bright as the day. Darkness and light are alike *to You*."

PSALM 139:7-8,11-12

So whether I choose a far road on my own volition, or whether I'm pressed into it by circumstances outside my control, either way He is somehow able to make *every* road, even the most difficult road, lead back toward Him.

When I look back on the seasons of my life when I felt the most distant, I now see that even my best efforts at hiding were not effective in keeping me from Him. He still came to find me.

To reclaim me.

To draw me back to Himself.

This is true for all of us. Just like it was true for Elijah.

Read the following verse and underline the spot where Elijah's journey led him after forty days of traveling through the wilderness.

Mount Horeb
is the same as
Mount Sinai.

He arose and ate and drank, and went in the strength of that food forty days and forty nights to Horeb, the mountain of God. Then he came there to a cave and lodged there.

1 KINGS 19:8-9a

Circle where you find Mount Horeb on your map.

Elijah's depression had grown so severe that he willingly launched himself into the vast, barren desert, six long weeks away from his last known stop. The location where he ended up was far south of where the rest of his travels had taken place. He couldn't have known at this point if he'd ever see another human being again or if he'd be able to survive the return trip, should he decide to head back.

This season of solitude is distinct from Elijah's time at Cherith, the dwindling brook where God specifically sent him and promised to provide for him. Fear and despondency were the only guides leading him into *this* desert, dictating his direction and actions. Clearly the tone of this portion of Elijah's story is a complete departure from the focused, purpose-filled journey thus far.

The Hebrew text reveals that Elijah went to "the" cave—presumably a reference to the cave of Moses.[1]

And yet God's redemptive purposes were still alive down here in the wilderness. This uncharted road will lead Elijah to an encounter with God that will reinvigorate, redirect, and refocus him. Here on this mountain, and here in this cave, he'll discover he can still hear God's voice and he can still participate in God's plan, despite the discouraged doubts that his effectiveness had come to a disparaging end. Yahweh can make sure that even a trip through the Sinai Desert will not have been in vain.

I'm so glad this segment of Elijah's story is included in Scripture, aren't you? It reminds me that God is there—ready and waiting for us—even when circumstances have redirected us or we have foolishly run into a wilderness of our own. In reality, this redemptive thread is what the Bible is all about, which is why evidences of it are scattered all over Scripture.

Choose two of the following biblical personalities for a short case study. Read the passage for each, and then answer the following questions:

- Hagar (Gen. 16:1-13)
- Jacob (Gen. 27:42-45; 28:10-22)
- Moses (Ex. 3:1-12)
- Gideon (Judg. 6:11-24; 7:16-21)
- Peter (Luke 22:54-62; Acts 2:32-36)
- Paul (2 Cor. 1:5-11)

- How would you describe their emotional state? Which words or phrases lead you to this conclusion?
- What setting or circumstances were they enduring that might have made them feel hopeless, despairing, and distant from God?
- How did they experience God and His character in a uniquely personal way?
- How did the person's life change as a result of this encounter?
- Of the two people you studied, which one did you most relate to? What elements of their story seem the most familiar to you, and why?

Pause and ask the Holy Spirit to personalize His Word in your life right now. Ask Him to open your spiritual eyes to see ways in which He is already present, and how He is turning your current wilderness into a highway toward Him. Below, record how you're sensing that He is redirecting you, changing you, revealing Himself to you, and repositioning you for something new.

My forty-fifth birthday was on December 31, 2019. My mother died in my arms the day before. I remember waking up on my birthday in a fog, not even remembering what date it was. To tell you the truth, the numb feeling continued for many months afterward. Unable to delay my own pending surgery, which I told you about, I was immediately thrust into a recovery process of another sort—my body's physical recovery, traveling directly alongside my soul's emotional recovery.

It was tough. On many fronts. I noticed, for example, that I had a hard time digesting new information. Or being mentally productive. Or fully engaging in the most regular and basic of life tasks, as well as staying focused on projects and endeavors that were once enjoyable activities. All the losses we'd endured in recent months had been difficult, but losing my own Mommy? It seemed to push me over the emotional edge. Overnight I felt as though I'd been thrust into a stagnant wilderness of exhaustion and numbness. And admittedly, like Elijah, I journeyed more deeply into it.

That's why this section in Elijah's story—along with that of Hagar and Jacob, Moses and Gideon, Peter and Paul, and a whole bunch of others—has really encouraged me. Their examples remind me that even when my paths are hurtful, disappointing, earth-shattering, or unexplainable, those same paths can still put me in prime position to experience God in a new way. To see Him from a new vantage point. To relate to Him and understand Him in a different, more mature, more dynamic way for the future.

The hound of heaven can find us no matter where we are.

"Am I a God at hand, declares the LORD, and not a God far away? Can a man hide himself in secret places so that I cannot see him? declares the LORD. Do I not fill heaven and earth? declares the LORD."

JEREMIAH 23:23-24, ESV

Mount Horeb is in this desert of yours, sis. And even here we'll find God waiting for us. Nothing we're walking through has the power to take us away from Him. Instead, inexplicably, we'll be drawn closer to Him. All the pain or sadness or disappointment we may feel in these difficult places won't disappear, but the hope of His presence will break our fall. It puts the brakes on despair. His presence is like a bungee cord that yanks us back from the perilous death spiral of utter hopelessness.

Be encouraged and know that even *this* road—the one that goes off the map—is a road that can lead you back to Him. I know it doesn't seem so, but because of His redemptive grace, you're actually headed in a direction brimming with the beauty and brilliance of a divine encounter. This road leads to the mountain of God.

And He is already there ahead of you.

Pray this:

Father, I am dry and lonely. I am tired and out of answers. I don't see how I'll ever get beyond this and feel right again about anything. But even though I do feel lost and rudderless right now, I believe—by faith—that You haven't lost **me.** *Thank You for being willing AND able to make this wilderness my next step in a new direction. You will lead me through it and meet me on the other side. In Jesus' name, amen.*

WHAT ARE YOU DOING HERE?

"[Elijah] came there to a cave and lodged there; and behold, the word of the LORD came to him, and He said to him, 'What are you doing here, Elijah?'"

1 KINGS 19:9

God is good at asking questions. And whenever He does, we can be sure He already knows the answer. Divine inquiries are never for our Father's benefit; He poses them with the intention of helping us see the truth of our situation, be honest with ourselves, and then agree with Him about His solution for us. God's questions require an authentic soul-searching to help us exhume issues of the heart that we hadn't formerly recognized or have been choosing to ignore. They make us dig deeply, beyond the surface layer of hurt and disappointment, past the veneer of happiness we've cleverly placed before others. By the time we've dealt with a question from God, He has shown us where we *really* are, and He has placed on the doorstep of our lives the next opportunity for us to mature in our faith and experience His power.

> Look at 1 Kings 19:9, as well as verse 13. Write down the identical question that Yahweh asked Elijah.

FOR GROUP DISCUSSION: Why do you think God may have asked Elijah two identical questions—first when Elijah came *into* the cave, and next when he was coming *out* of it?

Ask the Holy Spirit how this question applies to you right now in your life—spiritually, emotionally, and relationally. Before you fully launch into this lesson, invite Him to pierce through any superficial layers of denial or deflection you've erected, and to show you the particular truths He wants you to recognize about where you *really* are in any specific area and what got you there. Record below anything He brings to mind.

ELIJAH

God's pattern of asking questions began early in the pages of the Bible. Look up these passages from the lives of Adam and Eve and of Cain and Abel. Beside each reference write down the questions God asked.

- Genesis 3:6-11

- Genesis 4:3-7

- Genesis 4:8-10

Jesus, too, was a master at asking people questions during His ministry. The Gospels record dozens and dozens of them. Here are just a handful:

"Who do people say that the Son of Man is?"

MATTHEW 16:13

"But who do you say that I am?"

MATTHEW 16:15

"What do you want Me to do for you?"

MATTHEW 20:32

"How many loaves do you have?"

MARK 6:38

"What were you discussing on the way?"

MARK 9:33

"Who is the one who touched me?"

LUKE 8:45

"Do you wish to get well?"

JOHN 5:6

"Simon, son of John, do you love Me?"

JOHN 21:16

From these several examples, choose two or three and read the context surrounding them to consider what the Lord was actually trying to reveal to the person or persons He was addressing. What could it have compelled them to realize about themselves, their situation, or more importantly, their relationship to Him?

¹⁰ "I have been very zealous for the LORD God of Armies, but the Israelites have abandoned your covenant, torn down your altars, and killed your prophets with the sword. I alone am left, and they are looking for me to take my life. ¹¹ Then [God] said, "Go out and stand on the mountain in the LORD's presence." At that moment, the LORD passed by. A great and mighty wind was tearing at the mountains and was shattering cliffs before the LORD, but the LORD was not in the wind. After the wind there was an earthquake, but the LORD was not in the earthquake."

1 KINGS 19:10-11, CSB

For Elijah, Yahweh's question wasn't as much about addressing his geographical location; it was about the internal spiritual state that had driven him there. This holy question unearthed deep-seated realities that Elijah needed to address, and it cleared the way for his attention to be refocused, his hearing to be refined, and his path to be redirected.

As this scene unfolds in 1 Kings 19, it begins with a question designed to shift Elijah's perspective on himself and his prophetic ministry.

Take the time to read and savor this entire event in Elijah's life (1 Kings 19:11-21). We'll refer back to it throughout the remainder of today's lesson, as well as tomorrow, so keep your Bible nearby. After you finish reading, meet me back here.

Compare verses 10 and 11 in the margin, paying close attention to the highlighted portions. How does the main focus shift between the two verses? What is their noticeable difference in tone and emphasis?

Now compare Elijah's first response to the question in verse 10 with his response to the same question in verse 14. What insight does this discovery give you regarding how stubbornly embedded our self-deception can be?

God's question, in conjunction with the remarkable happenings soon to follow, are about to expose a mound of self-focused pity that had consumed Elijah's thinking. Yahweh's voice not only beckoned Elijah to come out of the dank, dark cave where he'd run and hidden himself away—not only to come out of there *physically*—but also to emerge spiritually, mentally, and emotionally from the self-obsession he'd allowed to overtake his whole outlook on life. All at once, with the surgical dexterity of one pinpointed question, God commanded His prophet to readjust his position and his focus, to walk out of the darkness in all regards, so that his vision could be set once again on the Lord.

We can attest, having spent six weeks in detailed study on the happenings that took place at Cherith, Zarephath, and Carmel, as well as the intensely personal interactions they necessitated, that Elijah's life had been marked by being consistently preoccupied with Yahweh's presence and purpose. Despite many earlier opportunities to exert a me-first, self-willed reaction toward God's challenging, uncomfortable demands, Elijah proved unshakable. His commitment to prayer carried him through the many difficult days and even more lonesome nights. His fixed focus on Yahweh kept him upright, kept him moving, or at times kept him sitting perfectly still, for whatever the word of the Lord called him to do at any given moment. His attention was always true north, single-minded, laser-focused on surrendering all personal rights and preferences to the greater good of God's plans for divine renewal. Whatever it cost.

But now, here at Horeb, things were different. With his spiritual gaze and eyesight lowered from heaven down to earth, with his emotions misdirected onto himself and his circumstances, Elijah had become a shell of whom he once was. Faith had taken a back seat to fear. Hope had been overshadowed by hopelessness. Expectancy had succumbed to dread.

ELIJAH, WHAT ARE YOU DOING *HERE*? HOW DID YOU GET *HERE*?

This is, in fact, the only outcome where the road of unrestrained introspection ever leads. The trajectory of a heart that's turned inwardly on itself cannot help but take a downward path. Becoming obsessed with ourselves is sure to lead toward a dramatic pitfall into fear and insecurity.

Take the example of Peter, for instance, when he saw Jesus walking on the water:

> "Peter said to Him, 'Lord, if it is You, command me to come to You on the water.' And He said, 'Come!' And Peter got out of the boat, and walked on the water and came toward Jesus. But seeing the wind, he became frightened, and beginning to sink, he cried out, 'Lord, save me!'"

MATTHEW 14:28-30

A misplaced focus, an overly sensitive concern with self or circumstances, changes everything. And it will consistently beg a question of God—even as it brought an attentive question from Jesus to Peter, as He "stretched out His hand and took hold of him, and said to him, 'You of little faith, why did you doubt?'" (v. 31).

Questions are simply God's way of reminding you to fix your eyes back on Him.

Another fitting example of this principle is the prophet Jonah. Turn to his Old Testament book and read through Jonah 4:1-4. Below, record the question that God asked the prophet.

Jonah was clearly displeased and angry that Yahweh had shown mercy to the vicious Ninevites. He'd hesitantly obeyed Yahweh's instructions to go there and preach about repentance, but he didn't really want them let off the hook of divine destruction.

Jonah 4:4 captures the first time God spoke in this chapter. It's almost as if He'd just been waiting on the prophet to finish his tirade of whining and complaining. In fact, the Masoretic text—the traditional, self-pronouncing Hebrew text of the Jewish Bible—places a *setumah* here, a grammatical device that punctuates the text with a pause when the story is read. Picture it playing out in real time: a father allowing his whiny child to ramble himself uninterrupted to the end of his complaints, and then—dead silence—a pause, just long enough to wonder what the father will do or say next. The suspense builds, and then Yahweh responds. Not with rebuke, not with silence, but with a probing question.

What do you think Yahweh's question was meant to cause Jonah to see about himself? About God?

> The LORD said, "Do you have good reason to be angry?"
>
> **JONAH 4:4**

Our God, see, has all the time in the world. He can wait us out and lovingly, carefully probe us by His Spirit and through His Word until we see Him and His perspective more clearly. Jonah couldn't move forward without dealing with the root of his anger, and Elijah couldn't move forward until he'd dealt with the root of his despair.

Neither can we. So, really, *What are you doing here?*

The Lord was there on the mountain with Elijah, and He is here today, too, to open us up to His revelation of truth—the truth about Him, about ourselves, about our circumstances, about everything. He has come to ask the kinds of questions that will draw us out of fear and self-pity so that we can "go forth and stand on the mountain" (1 Kings 19:11a) with a willingness to let God take us wherever He wants us to go.

Having come prayerfully to the end of today's lesson, talk to the Lord about what He wants to shift in you as a result of the answers that His questions are unearthing. Confess any ways that you've been overly focused on yourself or your circumstances. And now *fix your eyes back on Him.* Ask the Holy Spirit to help you throughout the next twenty-four hours to continually adjust your attention so that it is squarely situated on Jesus.

EARTH, WIND, AND FIRE

"Behold, the LORD was passing by!"

1 KINGS 19:11b

Many years ago, one of my mentors in the faith said something to me that I've never forgotten and has shaped my perspective for many years:

Priscilla, in your walk with the Lord, sometimes the greatest hindrance to a new move of God in your life can simply be an unhealthy preoccupation with a previous move of God in your life.

Right here at the beginning of your time with the Lord today, consider the statement you just read. What does it mean to you?

This precious woman's loving and gentle warning was clear. Sometimes we box God into the way He's done things in the past, and we presume He will always act or respond in that same way in the future. In doing so, however, we run an almost certain risk that we will miss seeing how God is moving in our lives today, right now, even as we embark on this final day of Bible study together.

> While God's character is sure and unchanging, His methods are at His divine disposal.
>
> **#ElijahBibleStudy**

For while God's character is sure and unchanging, His methods are at His divine disposal. Therefore we must keep our spiritual senses continually and progressively sharpened by *His* Spirit, so that we remain open and ready to experience Him in the way He wants. Our prior expectations and limited perspective do not place any boundaries around the way He chooses to work out His purposes, but they could limit our ability to perceive and relate to them. And we surely don't want to do *that*.

We arrive now at this culminating message from Elijah's encounter with Yahweh on Mount Sinai, also known as Horeb. It comes with heartfelt encouragement, but also with a course correction against this tendency for trying to make the work of God formulaic and predictable. I hope we'll emerge stirred with holy anticipation for what God has prepared for our lives in the weeks, months, and years to come.

Yesterday you read 1 Kings 19:11-21 in its entirety. Reread just the portion printed below, zeroing in on the various *elements of nature* that Elijah encountered on the mountain. Circle each one.

"[God] said, 'Go forth and stand on the mountain before the LORD.' And behold, the LORD was passing by! And a great and strong wind was rending the mountains and breaking in pieces the rocks before the LORD; but the LORD was not in the wind. And after the wind an earthquake, but the LORD was not in the earthquake. After the earthquake a fire, but the LORD was not in the fire; and after the fire a sound of a gentle blowing. When Elijah heard it, he wrapped his face in his mantle and went out and stood in the entrance of the cave."

1 KINGS 19:11-13a

Record the progression of Elijah's experience. The Lord was *not* in . . .

1.
2.
3.

The verses below chronicle other Old Testament instances when Yahweh had used similar elements to demonstrate His presence and power. Grab your Bible and look up each passage. For each one, select the corresponding letter from the list of natural elements that corresponds to each reference. (Some will be used more than once.)

- Exodus 3:2-3   A. Wind
- Exodus 10:13   B. Cloud
- Exodus 13:22   C. Fire
- Exodus 19:9
- 1 Kings 18:38

It's easy to hastily assume that a repeated event, a familiar emotional response, or a recognizable chain of incidents is a sure sign of God's presence and approval. Our human tendency is to respond to what we recognize while discounting what we've never experienced. But with the things of God, we must stay discerning and prayerful, seeking the Spirit's insight and the Scriptures' confirmation on every occasion. We don't want to lazily interpret the most commonly expected things as always being holy things. Sometimes, in fact, the Lord will allow us to walk through the wilderness for *this purpose alone*—to cleanse our spiritual palate, pique our spiritual senses, and compel us to seek Him with fresh interest and passion. To stay open to what He's doing now, doing next.

> Think back to a genuine encounter you've had with God. Is there any way you've inadvertently allowed that moment to become the prototype for how you assume He will move in the future? Every time?

"Know that
I am God."

PSALM 46:10b

> How has your takeaway from that experience caused you to become limited and narrow in your spiritual life?

Beloved sister, as you walk forward in your journey with the Lord, remember that His presence is not always characterized as something that thrills us—an emotional reaction that startles us; a big, bold event that awakens us; a flashy circumstance that wows us; or an eye-opening occurrence that surprises us. Just because it's extraordinary—just because it's cut from the earthquake, hurricane, or wildfire variety—doesn't automatically mean it's Him at work. Just because it's hyper doesn't mean it's holy. This misconception will inevitably blind us to the occasions when His authentic activity is in the "sound of a gentle blowing."

Look at the beautiful ways that Elijah's experience with God on Mount Sinai is rendered in different translations of the passage:

- "A low whisper" (ESV)
- "Sheer silence" (NRSV)
- "A gentle blowing" (NASB)
- "A still small voice" (KJV)
- "A soft whisper" (CSB)

How did Elijah respond when he heard it (v. 13)?

The contrast between the earthquake, the tumultuous wind, the searing fire, and the hushed, holy whisper of God is striking. The first three were loud and attention-getting; the last one was nearly imperceptible. But the contrast is symbolic of what God appeared to be doing in His continued work with the nation of Israel. As the stormy, volatile ministry of Elijah moved toward its conclusion, the relatively gentle ministry of his protégé, Elisha, was soon to dawn.

It was time for a stiller, smaller voice.

Detecting God's presence in these quieter ways requires patience and a keen spiritual ear, the kind He's been developing in you throughout every day of our Bible study together. And this sensitivity will continue to develop in you as you keep walking with Him and growing in grace. His voice will draw you out of the caves of despair, disillusionment, and discouragement and will usher you into a freedom and newfound reverence for Him, a renewed and hopeful outlook for the future—based on the certainty of His Word, of course, but not necessarily the same look and feel as you've been accustomed to equating with Him. Remain open to this.

The stillness of God's manifest presence drew Elijah to his feet. He wrapped his cloak over his face in reverence, and he came out to stand at the mouth of the cave. Then God spoke to him, giving him a new assignment and role in His divine purposes for the future.

Turn to 1 Kings 19:15-16. Wade through all the names there and boil it down to the three major directives that Yahweh gave Elijah.

1. Anoint _____ as king over Aram.
2. Anoint _____ as king over Israel.
3. Anoint _____ as prophet.

The beautiful lesson surging underneath this moment in Elijah's life—hearing the Lord speak to him in the "sheer silence"—is that God beckoned him to a new calling and method of ministry. This means Elijah's despondency had not disqualified him from being a key player in the goal of calling Israel back to allegiance to Yahweh. He was still a part of God's purpose, and, hallelujah, so are you!

So am I!

National revival had always been Elijah's divinely assigned objective, but the prophet had been pursuing this goal from one specific angle—the one in which *his* efforts alone accomplished the goal. He'd been obedient in his actions, but his presumption became the direct catalyst for his deep discouragement. He felt like he'd failed.

But now, God speaks again, here on Mount Horeb, clarifying to Elijah that despite his disappointment, he still has a key role to play. He was to anoint a specific new king over Aram (also known as Syria), as well as a specific new king over Israel, and was also to formally pass the baton to a new man who would carry on the prophetic mantle that Elijah had carried so diligently and faithfully. The combined efforts of these individuals would be strategic in bringing Ahab and Jezebel's rule to a sure end and spurring Israel toward the unhindered worship of Yahweh that they'd been redeemed to enjoy.

God's work would still be done; it just wouldn't all be done by Elijah. His prophetic assignment was not yet over, but it was now time—in God's time—for his ministry to be redirected. In this wilderness, and in that still small voice, God was telling Elijah that he continued to be significant to the Lord's divine purposes.

Sister, you are still significant to the fulfillment of God's plan. No matter your age or demographic, your temperament, or your previous disappointments, the breath filling your lungs right now is an indicator that He still considers you a necessary part of what He's advancing and accomplishing on the earth. There is nothing (and I do mean *nothing!*) that has rendered you useless or expendable to Him. Just don't let your expectations about how your part is supposed to look or how God will reveal it to you discourage you from being yielded and available for what He is asking you to do right now.

Modern-day Elijah, be faithful.

Don't give up.

There's work to be done.

He's whispering to you even now, giving you new direction, new insight, and fresh encouragement. He's reminding you that He still has a divine plan with generational implications, and this plan involves *you*—running full speed ahead, even if it takes you down a path you weren't anticipating, and then passing the baton of faith along to others who will run alongside you, as well as beyond you.

This, too, is the legacy of Elijah. Not just fire, not just Mount Carmel. Elijah's legacy includes this much-needed reminder that less-flashy work is no less God's work. And that the later days of one's life and ministry can still be fruitful, effective, important, valuable parts of what God wants done in this generation. Not only can still be, but *need* to be.

Elijah's story is God's story, just as your story and my story are God's story. The process He takes us through, as well as the pinnacles he takes us to, show us He doesn't want us left out of the mission He's working to accomplish. He is always getting us ready for what's next. And there is always something next, something here, something *now* that He's been preparing you to do—through the growing times, through the waiting times, through the up times, even through the down times. These are *our* times—this is *your* time.

Shhhhh. Listen.

The Lord is passing by.

> You are still significant to the fulfillment of God's plan.
>
> #ElijahBibleStudy

Heavenward

FAITH, FAILURE, AND BEYOND

#ELIJAHBIBLESTUDY

WEEK SEVEN

FAITH, FAILURE, AND A FUTURE

God knew all these things, _____ them all in, and still _____ us to be _____ for His _____.

Every time we see their failures, it should underscore the fact that we are looking for a _____, that we need somebody else to be our _____.

He has _____ been and will always be the _____, the _____, and the _____.

Video and audio sessions available for purchase and rent at LifeWay.com/Elijah.

217

SESSION ONE

DISCUSSION STARTER: After meeting others in the group, encourage women to discuss what drew them to participate in this study on Elijah. Bearing in mind that some participants may be new to the Bible and not as familiar with his story, ask what the group considers to be the highlights of his ministry and legacy. Talk through your and their expectations for the study.

READ HEBREWS 5:14 as an introduction to our need for "practice" or "training" in the development of Christian maturity. Knowing the importance of training in other areas of life (physically, academically, vocationally), discuss why we don't as naturally think we need seasons of training for developing our faith also. Ask why we assume people who exhibit a robust faith, like Elijah, just simply know how to do it.

WATCH THE WEEK ONE VIDEO: "The Start of a Process"

• Discuss our tendency to put people on pedestals, to think of their "highlight reels" as representing the full story about them.

• What do you want your life to portray about the power of God, at work in an ordinary person?

• Ask the group to deal personally with the question: "Am I willing to do what Elijah did to get what Elijah got?"

CLOSE IN PRAYER.

SESSION TWO

DISCUSSION STARTER: Review the account of Elijah's appearance before King Ahab in 1 Kings 17:1. Imagine the novelty of someone coming from the backwoods, like Elijah did, meeting with the king, getting to see how things work at the center of power. Ask the women to share a similarly exciting experience from their own lives. How hard would it be, though, having seen God make your ministry influence so public, to now accept an assignment that took you back into obscurity?

READ MARK 8:34-35, where Jesus defines the heart of a disciple. What does He promise to those who forsake their own wants and wishes in exchange for choosing to follow Him, wherever He says to go?

WATCH THE WEEK TWO VIDEO: "Preparation by Separation"

• Imagine being called by God, like Elijah, into a season of separation, all by yourself. How would you most likely spend your time? What would your choices reveal? How can you apply these same lessons toward any sort of separation God might be calling you to make?

• Ask your group to notice the timing of God's provision for him at Cherith. Did the ravens come *before* or *after* he'd been obedient in going there, in following through on God's assignment for him? How many of our doubts about God's willingness to provide for us are perhaps tied to our own unwillingness to go where He's waiting to show it to us?

ASK FOR A VOLUNTEER TO CLOSE YOUR TIME IN PRAYER.

SESSION THREE

DISCUSSION STARTER: *Out of the frying pan, into the fire.* That's what we'll see happening in Elijah's life this week, as he follows God's itinerary from the dry gulch of Cherith to the furnace of Zarephath. Ask your group how they typically handle life when it feels like that, when it seems to be going from bad to worse.

READ EPHESIANS 3:20-21, having several members of the group read it in different translations of the Bible. Focus on the phrase: "above all that we ask or think." Invite volunteers to share the testimony they recalled during their individual study this week, a memorable time when God's care for their needs went above and beyond what they thought possible.

WATCH THE WEEK THREE VIDEO: "Dealing with Deficiency"

- What do you find most astounding about Elijah's faith and demeanor during this period of his life?

- What do you find most appealing or interesting about the widow's reaction to the challenges she was facing?

AS A GROUP, PRAY SPECIFICALLY FOR GOD'S HELP IN APPLYING THE FOUR INSIGHTS PRISCILLA UNPACKED ON THE SUBJECT OF "HOW TO DEAL WITH DEFICIENCY."

SESSION FOUR

DISCUSSION STARTER: The past week has been a time for considering how being outside of your comfort zone can, in Priscilla's words, "reshape your perspectives, refine your behaviors, and reframe your attitudes." Ask the women to share how they've noticed this kind of growth and deepening in their own lives— the result of times when God has taken them to places they didn't want to go.

READ 2 PETER 1:5-8. As you come to each character trait in this progressive list, talk about your longing to grow in that area (in "knowledge," for example—in "self-control," in "endurance"). Ask if the women's desire for these characteristics— each of which builds on "faith" (v. 5) —is worth whatever God might know is required to produce it in them.

WATCH THE WEEK FOUR VIDEO: "Don't Drop the Ball"

- Obadiah's story is a reminder that God places people in all kinds of spheres where He expects them to use their skills and influence for His purposes. Ask the group to share how men and women in everyday, secular positions have impacted and inspired them in their Christian faith.

- What are some of the pressing areas of challenge in today's world, or simply in your own life, where you most want to be sure you "don't drop the ball"? How might you need to adjust your activities and priorities to be sure you're clearly focused on what really matters?

PRAY FOR EACH INDIVIDUAL WOMAN IN YOUR GROUP. ASK GOD TO INSTILL IN HER THE COURAGE AS WELL AS THE ABILITY TO PUT HER FAITH INTO LIVING PRACTICE.

SESSION FIVE

DISCUSSION STARTER: "How long will you waver between two opinions?" (1 Kings 18:21). This was the line Elijah drew in the sand on Mount Carmel. It's the same line we cross every morning on our way to deciding how we'll live each day. How did you answer the following question this week: "What makes being a nominal, tepid follower of Jesus more convenient and acceptable in today's culture?" Where do these temptations toward compromise show no signs of stopping—in our own lives, our kids' lives, and the generation coming up behind us?

READ ROMANS 13:11-14. What does Paul say it's time for God's people to do? Where do you most feel the need to "wake up"? What are the idols in your life that have been making it too easy for you to get drowsy in your devotion to the Lord?

WATCH THE WEEK FIVE VIDEO: "Inviting the Fire"

• What's distinctive about the fire of God? Why is generating His fire never up to us, to our initiative and ability? And yet, what are three practical investments of faith that invite His holy fire? Which of them strikes you as being the most needed, the most desired and sought after in your life?

• Recall again the many steps of obedience Elijah took on his way to this mountaintop experience on Carmel. How was each of them instrumental in preparing him for this moment? How does witnessing his faith and boldness on this incredible day encourage you to make the absolute most of your own day—this day—another day in God's process with you?

CLOSE IN PRAYER. PRAY FOR FIRE.

SESSION SIX

DISCUSSION STARTER: One of the most difficult challenges for Elijah on Mount Carmel, as we observed this week, was that he not only needed to step out alone against the prophets of Baal but also step out alone from among his own people. Discuss with each other how your group—this particular group of women—could commit to encouraging one another to be bold, ever bolder, in your faith, never a dampener of each others' desire to follow Christ with fearless abandon.

READ DEUTERONOMY 12:1-3. Reinforce the teaching from the final day of the week concerning the complete destruction of our idols. Ask volunteers to call out some of the action verbs from this passage in Deuteronomy, describing what God expected to be done with the altars and images of false gods in the land of Israel. Talk about how we often don't see the harm they're causing until they've become too embedded to be removed without pain. How could your group be an aid in helping kill off each others' idols as well?

WATCH THE WEEK SIX VIDEO: "Do You Hear What I Hear?"

• Share with the group a verse or promise from Scripture that the Spirit has illuminated recently in your life and how it's impacted you. Encourage others to share their own. Talk about how God often spotlights these things not only for our personal benefit but as a way for us to proclaim His truth to others and glorify Him in our conversations.

ELIJAH

- Why do we tend to pray without then *looking* for how God will respond, without actively *preparing* for what He is going to do? The answer to this question, like the answer to most questions of Christian life, is *faith*. Tie it all back with your group to the preparation process. God walks us through those seasons of challenge and difficulty to hone our *faith*, so that we're steadily growing in what it takes to be a conduit of His *fire*. Let's not waste those moments on anything else.

ASK A GROUP MEMBER TO PRAY FOR YOUR LAST WEEK OF STUDY.

SESSION SEVEN

DISCUSSION STARTER: In this past week of individual study, we've seen a different side to Elijah's personality. Ask the women to talk about their wonder that God would include such revealing, unflattering portraits of a biblical hero. More personally, ask them how they've been specifically encouraged, being able to relate with Elijah's own moodiness and struggle.

READ 1 KINGS 19:9,13. Reflect from your study why you believe God would ask the identical question of Elijah at either end of his time in the cave. What are some of the simple yet probing questions that God might be asking of you and the women these days?

WATCH THE WEEK SEVEN VIDEO: "Faith, Failure, and a Future"

- Lead the women in prayer. Ask that we all, in being taught by Elijah, would be drawn to desire Jesus more than anything.

- As you finish your time together, invite women to share what they consider the key takeaways God's Spirit has established in their hearts from this season of studying Elijah. Encourage them to be patient in the process, not hurrying themselves through seasons that are of necessary duration for the establishment of their faith. Encourage them, too, in any decision—from the most daily to the most life-altering—to always choose obedience. Remind them that faith like Elijah's doesn't just happen. But, praise God, He is working with us right this minute to make our own faith even stronger. Promise to keep up with each other and with each others' progress, and to keep inviting God's fire into your lives.

CLOSE IN PRAYER.

ENDNOTES

WEEK ONE

1. F. B. Meyer, *The F. B. Meyer Collection, Elijah and the Secret of His Power*, preface.

2. *The F. B. Meyer Collection, Elijah*, chapter 1.

3. "*Yehovah*," Strong's H3068, *Blue Letter Bible* online. Available at www.blueletterbible.org.

WEEK TWO

1. "Cherith," *Holman Bible Dictionary* (Nashville, TN: Holman Bible Publishers, 1991), 247.

2. *The F. B. Meyer Collection, Elijah*, chapter 2.

3. "Wadi," *Holman Bible Dictionary*, 1398.

4. Ray Pritchard, *Fire and Rain: The Wild-Hearted Faith of Elijah* (Nashville: B&H Publishing, 2007), 55.

5. Gene A. Getz, *Men of Character: Elijah: Remaining Steadfast Through Uncertainty* (Nashville: B&H, 1995), 36.

WEEK THREE

1. "Zarephath," *Holman Bible Dictionary*, 1433.

2. F. B. Meyer, *Elijah, and the Secret of His Power*, Chapter 5, "The Test of the Homelife."

WEEK FOUR

1. "*Pacach*," Strong's H6452, *Blue Letter Bible* online. Available at www.blueletterbible.org.

2. Terence E. Fretheim, *First and Second Kings* (Louisville, KY: Westminster Jon Knox Press, 1999), 102.

3. *Fire and Rain*, 109.

4. R. B. Coote (ed.), *Elijah and Elisha in Socioliterary Perspective* (Atlanta: Society of Biblical Literature, 2003), 10.

5. *Fire and Rain*, 111.

WEEK FIVE

1. Elisabeth Elliot, *The Path of Loneliness* (Grand Rapids, MI: Revell, 1998), 153.

2. The F. B. Meyer Collection, *Elijah*, chapter 8.

3. F. E. Marsh, *Emblems of the Holy Spirit* (Grand Rapids, MI: Kregel, 1981), 114–115.

WEEK SIX

1. Jeff Lucas, *Elijah: Anointed and Stressed* (Eastbourne, UK: Kingsway Publications, 1995), 121.